LEAD GUITAR WORKSHOP

Lead Guitar: Level 1

L.G.W
LEAD GUITAR WORKSHOP

Library of Congress Control Number:

Any references to historical events, real people, or real places are used fictitiously. Names, characters, and places are products of the author's imagination.

Front cover image by Suke Cerulo
Book design by Suke Cerulo
Front Cover photo by Jessica Maceli
About Author photo by Paul Citone
Student Reviewer Linda Ameroso

Printed by Lead Guitar Workshop, Inc., in the United States of America.

First edition 2021.

SCAN FOR MORE

for all backing tracks and videos

www.LeadGuitarWorkshop.com

PREFACE

I always enjoyed music as a kid but my immediate family was not musical. There wasn't a lot of music playing in the house and we were never the type of family to sing. But my Grandfather George Lane was a Big Band musician and bandleader in the 1950's in Boston and New York. I don't have any memories of him playing music but he would have hilarious stories "from the road" traveling with the band. Later in life I really learned to appreciate them as I toured extensively.

It was 1984 and I heard Van Halen for the first time. I knew right then and there that I wanted to play music. I got my first guitar for Christmas in that year and quickly took lessons because I had no idea what to do. At the time I was really into playing football and I was good at it. I realized I was never going to be in the NFL or make a career out of it. But I did realize there was no NFL of music, anybody could play! That was so exciting. I knew I was going to play music for my whole life. I just had to figure out how to make it a career.

I had weekly guitar lessons from the time I was twelve until I graduated High School. For most of this time my teacher was Sandy Prager. He played "third stream jazz" on a nylon string guitar. This was as far away from Van Halen as possible without being a classical guitarist. But I learned so much about music, how to think about it and improvise. He constantly had me creating. Once I finished High School I went to **Berklee College of Music**. It was the only school I wanted to go to. After four years I got my Bachelors Degree in Professional Music.

My one goal upon graduating was to join a band. Fortunately for me I met my future bandmates of 30 plus years. We formed the band "**Schleigho**" in 1993 and toured full time within a year or so. We toured 200 plus dates a year for almost five years straight and still play to this day. We recorded and released 5 albums. We signed a label with the **Allman Brothers Band**, toured with **Derek Trucks**, and played with so very many people all over the country. This was my "real world" music education.

But even though I had lessons in High School and a great experience at Berklee I still felt like I was slow learning and still really didn't get the true nature of music and guitar. I struggled to connect the musical dots.

I had to build confidence to make my own conclusions about music. I heard so many different ideas, terms, explanations and they were confusing. I was perplexed that music had been around for hundreds of years and there was still so much indecision about ideas and terminology.

I had to separate music from the instrument. This was one of my biggest realizations. It came into fruition when I started playing flute. I realized the music was its own language independent of the instrument that plays it. When I started really practicing flute my guitar playing got better! I was stunned, but I realized my musicianship was better and it was now translating to guitar.

Once my band started touring I had guitar players (and flute players) asking me for lessons. I think I gave my first lesson in 1995. It was very casual and it was new to me but I was just trying to help people out. I realized I had a good way of explaining things and I was able to connect with people. Over the years I kept teaching. It was rewarding and I was learning a lot by having to explain music to people in many different ways.

About six months after I moved to NYC in 2003 I got my first real teaching job at a guitar school in NYC. I was touring and teaching full time. I was engulfed in playing and teaching music and it was wonderful. As touring slowed down the teaching picked up. I was teaching ten classes and about thirty private students. Close to eighty folks a week were coming to see me to learn about guitar and music. After years of teaching groups and private students I was able to refine my approach to teaching and to understanding music and how it relates to the guitar. Years ago I estimated that I hit my 10,000 hours as a guitar player. Now I was hitting my 10,000 hours as a teacher.

In 2003 I wrote my first book "Lead Guitar Basics" for me to use at the guitar school. Over the years this grew into five complete books and a number of rewrites. I also became the Director of the Lead Guitar Department. I train other teachers to teach my material and musically evaluate all incoming teachers to the school.

I was amassing an unprecedented amount of teaching experience and gaining access to hundreds, if not thousands, of guitar players struggling in the same way I had. Over years of refinement I was able to develop this entire pedagogy for learning lead guitar.

These books have three decades of experience behind them and seventeen years of in-classroom development. I believe in these books, and I think they will help you immensely as you become a better guitarist and musician. These are all the things I wish I had when I was starting my journey.

HOW TO USE BOOK

Each book is written as ten lessons continually building on each other. The books all work together and are meant to extend and expand your knowledge as you work and grow with them. Go through them in order and go back later to revisit topics.

These books were initially created as 10 week courses, one chapter per week. You can use it in the same way. Each Chapter is about an hour long. There are enough warm-ups, exercises, new skills and practice to last you for a week. There is overlap and repetition in the books to really help reinforce the core ideas.

Every lesson is structured the same way. It is meant to optimize your learning, efficiency, and time. The repetition creates good habits.

Tune in: First you have to get in the right head space. You must remind yourself that you are a musician and a guitar player. That music is Melody, Harmony, and Rhythm; and that rhythm is the number one factor to sounding good. It's like a mantra.

Warm-up: These are exercises to get your musical blood flowing and synchronize your internal clock. There are usually up to three warm-ups; *Muted String Ladders*, *Shells*, and *Changing Gears*. They are all music based and are like push-ups and jumping jacks to athletes.

Exercises: These are straight up music exercises like scales, arpeggios and more.

Review: This is part of the learning circle. You must review everything you learn. Eventually that will become part of your everyday language.

New Topic: Learn something new. It can be big or small, but it should expand your knowledge, even if it's learning something new about something you already know.

Practice: Play! Get better by playing music. Use your new idea/technique, concept in real time in the music you are playing, even if it is a one chord jam by yourself. Self Generating music and backing tracks are a focal point.

Summary: A reminder of what has been learned so far. Summaries compound with each chapter.

Going through each word and each note as written in these books is only part of the bigger picture. You have to imagine how music is working and how it relates to your instrument. You have to have a desire to grow and a never ending curiosity about music. If you keep questioning music you will find more answers and go deeper and deeper. You have to "drive" music, start a song yourself, jam on it and make it music all by yourself. When you're playing by yourself and someone walks in they should ask you "What song are you playing?" not "What are you practicing?" Learning music and playing is not about checking off a list of requirements. It's about sounding like a musician playing good music, and not someone noodling at the guitar store.

At a certain point in your musical life, you will learn all the information about music that you will ever use. Then your growth is about becoming closer to that information and growing deeper with it every time you revisit it. There isn't a learning path in music, it's a learning circle. An ever expanding circle is like rings in a tree. It's the growth in the rings, in the trunk of the tree that allows those branches to grow and extend.

Music is just a language and a guitar is just an instrument. Both are silent without you, you are music!

As guitarists Pat Martino and Mike Stern both told me, and I will tell you, "Just keep playing." Enjoy!

Suke Cerulo

TABLE OF CONTENTS

Lead Guitar-Level 1

WHO IS THIS BOOK FOR?

This book is for beginning and intermediate guitar players who want to learn to play lead. This book is for those who have only played chords and songs and never played a solo. It's also for players who have soloed but want to start from the ground up with a method and workflow that builds a solid foundation for musicianship and playing guitar.

CHAPTER 1

TUNE IN

Whenever you grab your guitar you are dealing with two worlds. One is the language of music and the other is craft of the instrument. Each are different but necessary for music to exist.

Music is the language of notes, chords and rhythms, all independent of any instrument. The language of music has its own questions and answers. "What are the chords to this song?" "What key are we in?" What are the notes in the scale?" "How fast is this song?" The language of music is hundreds of years old, older than the guitar. It is a fixed language, and there are only 12 notes.

A musical instrument is just a tool we use to translate our language into vibrations of air molecules so we can hear and experience music. Each instrument has limits but unique abilities. For example, the human voice is only capable of singing one note-at-a-time; the guitar can play a maximum of 6 notes simultaneously; and the piano has the potential for 88 notes at one time.

Music: Music is the art of combining sounds and rhythms to produce a pleasing aural effect through the elements of melody, harmony, rhythm, and timbre (instrument).

Instrument (musical): A device that can produce the notes of the music language using vibrations.

<u>Timbre:</u> The character or quality of a musical sound or voice, separate from its pitch. It is the "tone" of the note. It helps each musical instrument playing the same note sound different.

<u>Melody:</u> A series of single tones (notes), one at a time, to produce a pleasing sound. It is the signature of a song. Notes are akin to a letter in the alphabet. Notes cannot be Major or minor but can be sharp (#) or flat (b). For guitar players these notes are our scales and arpeggios.

<u>Harmony:</u> Multiple notes played simultaneously to produce a chord (akin to a word in language). The two fundamental types of chords are Major and minor chords (There are more, for example 7th and diminished chords). These are our chords on guitar (open, bar, any others).

<u>Rhythm:</u> Rhythm is the measured flow of notes/attacks; the heartbeat/life blood of all music. A language independent of melody and harmony, Rhythm is everything; your foot tap, your strumming, and picking.

Rhythm is the number one factor to sounding great as a musician.

"You can have music with no melody (just chords), and you can have music with no harmony (just melody), but you cannot have music without rhythm. As soon as a note is played, rhythm exists. Rhythm is time."

"I am a musician and a guitar player. Music is my language and my guitar is my voice. Music is Melody, Harmony and Rhythm. I develop my language skills and my instrument skills. They are two separate worlds working together to complete the circle of music."

Can music exist without instruments?
Can instruments exist without music?

RHYTHM

All rhythm starts with, and is relative to, a beat. The common feeling everyone shares when music is playing, when you tap your foot, is the Beat. Usually this "foot tap" is know as a QUARTER-NOTE in music.

The quarter-note can happen at different speeds. This is known as TEMPO. Tempo is measured in Beats-per-minute (BPM). A foot tap every second would also be thought of as a QUARTER-NOTE at 60 BPM. A quarter-note is a 1:1 ratio of note/attack per foot tap.

Attack: any occurrence in time; hand clap, snap, click, footstep, stomp, beep, anything! Rhythm is everywhere. Rhythm is time itself.

An EIGHTH-NOTE is a 2:1 relationship to the beat. There are two notes/attacks evenly spaced per beat.

BAR/MEASURE: is a container for beats. Usually there are 4 beats per bar in a standard 4/4 time signature.

We count quarter-notes as **1 2 3 4.**

We count eighth-notes as **1+2+3+4+** (+ = "and").

We count each BAR as *one* 2 3 4, *two* 2 3 4, *three* 2 3 4, *four* 2 3 4.

METRONOME

Even though most people have a good sense of time we should always welcome an opportunity to use a timekeeper. The easiest is a METRONOME. It is your friend and the simplest drum beat in the world. You simply need a steady click and the ability to change the tempo. Most metronome apps have a TAP feature, allowing you to tap the screen in-time with a song and it will show you the tempo. It's great to get to know tempos. Most Hip Hop/R+B is around 88 BPM, and Headbangers around 96 BPM. Most POP songs are 120 BPM (aka the producers beat). These are just some common practices and by no means the rule. But it's a great idea to get to know the tempos of your favorite music.

ALL MUSIC IS RELATIVE TO RHYTHM. YOU MUST PLAY MUSIC IN TIME.

PICKING

As Guitar players we have two picking directions, DOWN and UP.
We have to get comfortable with both of them similar to a drummer getting comfortable with Left and Right hand combinations. The DOWN pick/strum will always be easiest and sound strong. The opposite is true for UP picks/strums. The goal is to get both actions as close to each other in terms of tone, volume, and control.

When playing, you should focus on the music and getting the right note, at the right time, with the right tone.

Here are the universal symbols for up and down pick/strums. They are adapted from old violin bowings. The down symbol is the blunt end of the bow, called the frog and the up pick symbol is the tip of the bow.

DOWN pick   UP pick

PICK HAND

Although there are many approaches to how to hold a pick, there are a few things to consider. Your hand should make a "mouth puppet" and put the pick in the curl of the index (1st) finger. This should create a 90 degree angle between your arm and downward point of the pick. Your remaining fingers will curl into a semi-closed grip. Choke up on the pick to only leave a small amount of the tip sticking out.

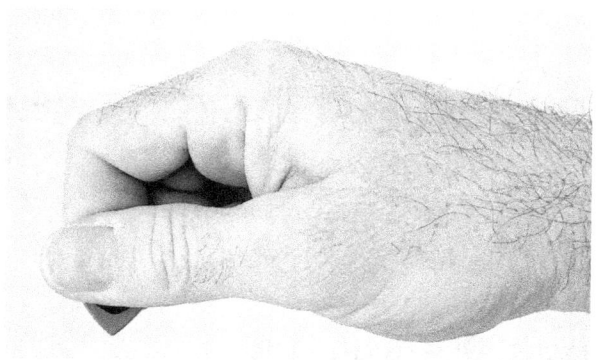 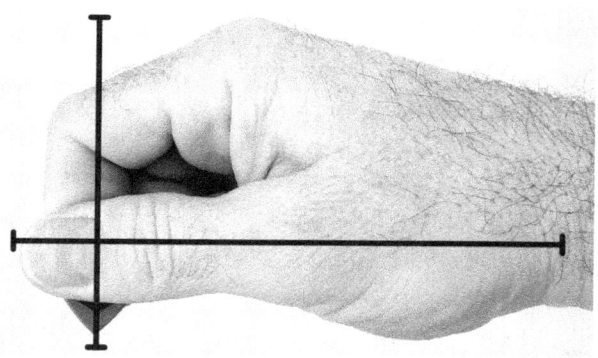

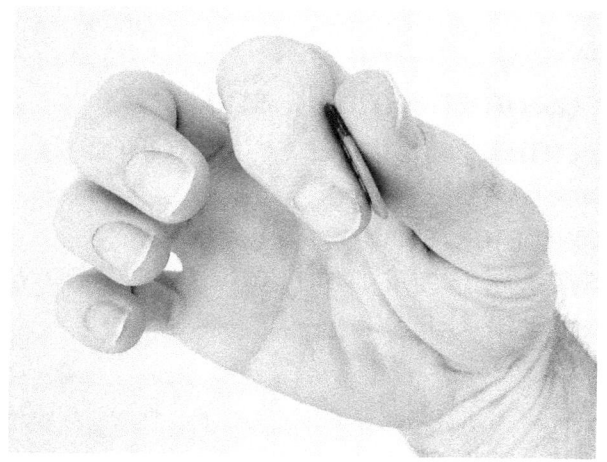 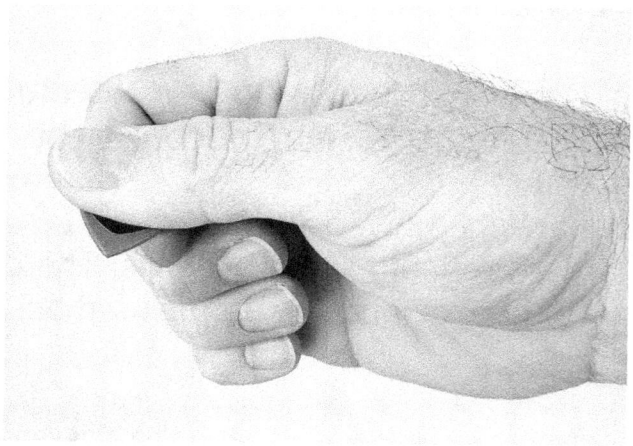

FRETBOARD HAND

There are two basic methods for grabbing the guitar with your fretboard hand. One is a traditional grip and one is sometimes referred to as the Blues grip. It's important to understand the benefits (and shortcomings) of each and be comfortable doing both.

When playing in the open position on the guitar (first 3 frets including the open strings) you will most likely be in a Blues grip. This means the thumb is over the top side of the neck and the grip feels like your grabbing a handle. Once you move up the neck and start doing bar chords, power chords and scales you will most likely adopt the traditional grip. This puts the thumb behind the first 2 fingers on the neck. This should feel like you're pulling down a shade. You will notice when in a Blues grip the fingers collapse on each other compared to the traditional grip in which the fingers have space in between allowing greater reach and abilities.

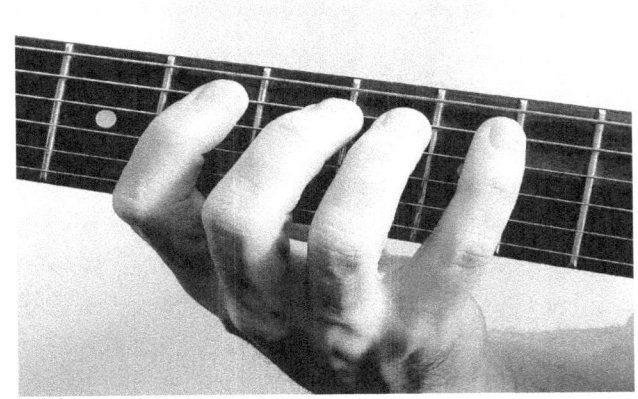 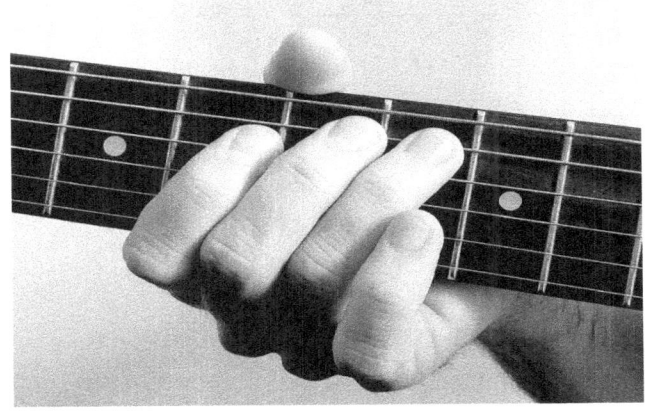

TRADITIONAL "STANCE"	BLUES
Better reach, allows a finger per fret x4	Better for bends
Better for Hammer-ons and Pull-off's	Better for OPEN position
Better for barring (2-6 strings at once)	Limited range of motion
Hard to bend	Hard to use pinky
Better for speed	Better for mute/strums (ala Stevie Ray Vaughn)
NOTE: bigger space between fingers	*NOTE: less space between fingers*

MUTED STRING LADDERS (MSL)

This is a pick hand exercise to help develop great rhythm and pick control. It requires using your fretboard hand to lightly press on the strings to mute them. (We want all of our focus on the picking hand.) You should repeat each bar a minimum of 8 times before moving to next one.

Your picking hand will pick the strings in 3 different ways:
ALL UP picked, then ALL DOWN picked, and finally ALL ALTERNATE picked.

The number of strings used can vary and so can the rhythm.

MSL Single string   Quarter-notes   60 BPM

MSL Single string   eighth-notes   60 BPM

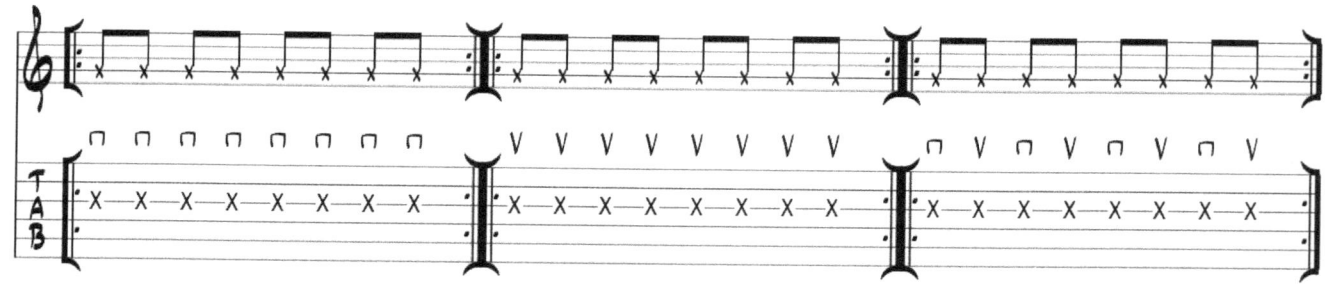

SHELLS

This is an exercise that helps the two hands work together in a musical way to help overcome shortcomings in the hand's abilities to play any combination of notes. These are like my "Wax on, Wax off" (Karate Kid). Shells can also be thought of as push-ups or jumping jacks. All athletes do them to help with everything else they do.

The SHELL has three parts to it:

1-FINGERINGS: Choose any combo of fingers 1 2 3 4 and pick a starting fret.

2-PERFORMANCE: Play "in position" (staying on the same frets).

3-RHYTHM: Choose a rhythm. (Like everything, shell exercises need a rhythm, for example quarter-notes or eighth-notes.)

SHELL PRINCIPAL:

Whatever fingering you choose,
Play it **THE SAME WAY** *ascending + descending*.
Then <u>REVERSE</u> the **order of the fingers**
and play it **THE SAME WAY** *ascending + descending*.

PENTATONIC SCALES

Pentatonic scales are five note scales that have been part of human culture for hundreds of years. They are much older than the guitar itself. There are two fundamental types/sounds of pentatonic scales. One is Major and one is minor.

The Major pentatonic scale is a very happy and upbeat sounding scale. It is 5 notes of our traditional seven note scale. It utilizes the 1 2 3 5 6 notes of a scale. If you ever learned Do Re Me Fa So La Ti Do, then it would be Do, Re, Me, So, and La.

The G Major pentatonic scale would be **G A B D E.**

As a guitar player we use scale patterns and TAB to help locate scales. Here is one octave G Major pentatonic scale on the guitar notated in a scale diagram. The highest note is the G on the 3rd fret of the high E string. The lowest note is the open G string. Scales move in a zig-zag fashion on the fretboard, making it hard to visualize the true up and down of the scale. Don't forget to use your ears and listen to it.

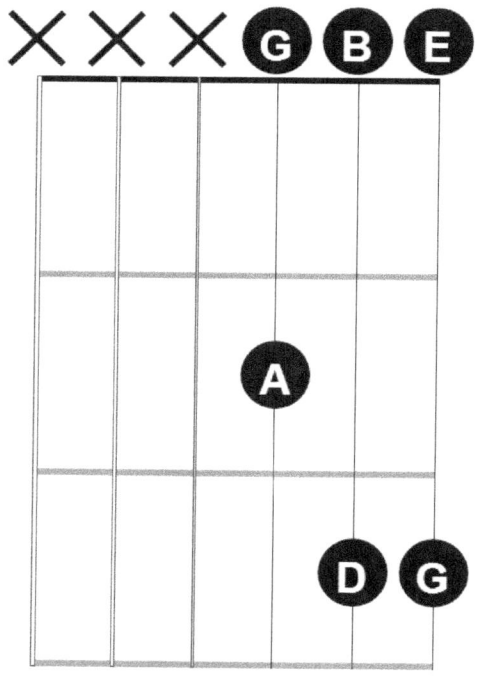

Here is the scale written in TAB.

DESCENDING QUARTER-NOTES

ASCENDING QUARTER-NOTES

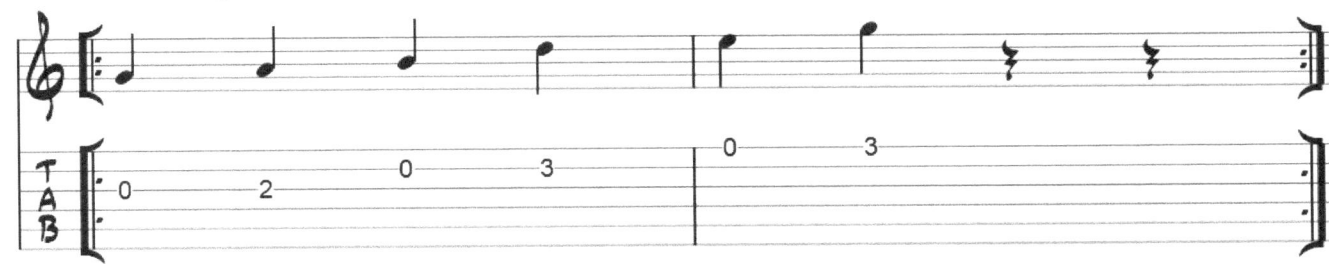

DESCENDING EIGHTH-NOTES

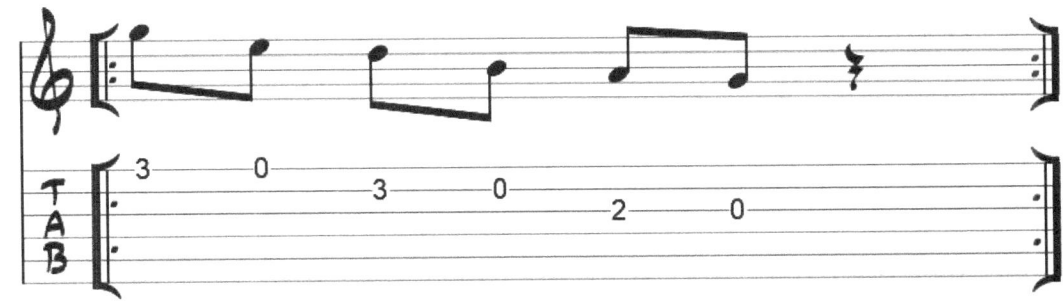

ASCENDING EIGHTH-NOTES

PRACTICE

1. Set metronome to 60 BPM.
2. Play the scale ascending and descending as quarter-notes.
3. Play the scale ascending and descending as eighth-notes.

Old School TIP: Strum G Major chord, play scale, strum G chord again. This helps give your ear a reference to the notes.

LICKS

A lick is a slang term for a handful of notes that sound cool. They can be based on a genre of music, with sounds and moves common to that style. (For example, compare a Country guitar lick to a blues lick.) They can be based by player, a phrase that a musician might use a lot in their music. (For example, an Eric Clapton lick from song x). Licks are NOT static snapshots of music, but flexible and malleable phrases able to adapt and morph into many other sounds. Licks are building blocks to other licks and even more complete musical phrases.

G MAJOR LICK 1

Quarter-notes

Eighth-notes

G MAJOR LICK 2

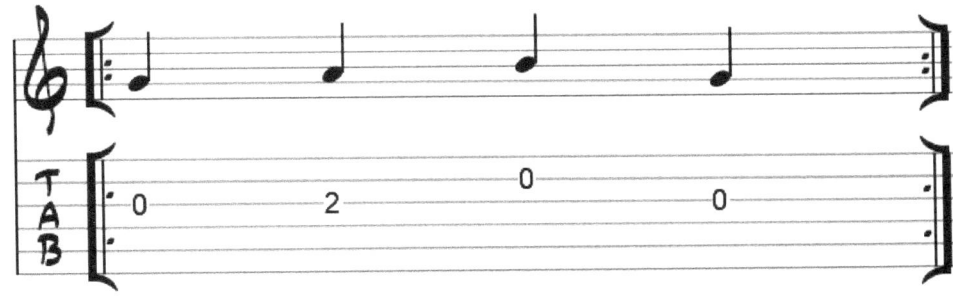

Quarter-notes

Eighth-notes

BACKING TRACKS

Backing Tracks are one of the best ways to practice lead guitar. First, they are a time keeper. There is a drum beat and a groove. They also have chords, which are necessary for scales to sound properly. Chords provide a harmonic backdrop to give context and color to the melody notes (solo). You can practice the scales over backing tracks, and you can play licks over the backing tracks and eventually solo.

HOW TO CHOOSE A SCALE

We make our music decisions first and then go to our instrument.

First we need to know the chords of our song, or of the section of the song we are going to solo over.

Then we decide which chord is the "Main" chord. (The "main" chord is not necessarily the Key we are in, although it often is the same). We need to find which one of these chords sounds like "home." (Which chord does it come to rest on? Which chord would you end on if you were playing it at a concert.

Strum the chord progression below a few times and you will realize that the G chord is the "Main" chord.

Now as a MUSICIAN we match a G Major Chord with a G Major Pentatonic scale. This is global. The scale for the main chord should work for all the chords. This is playing globally.

As a Guitar player we know a 1 octave G Major pentatonic scale in the open position.

$\frac{4}{4}$|G |D |Em |C   ‖

For the follow-along BACKING TRACK VIDEO visit
www.LeadGuitarWorkshop.com

SUMMARY

You are a guitar player and musician. You are learning two separate worlds, the music language and guitar as an instrument.

Music is Melody Harmony and Rhythm. Rhythm is most important.

To improve on our instrument we warm up with Muted String Ladders and Shells.

As a musician we learned about the G Major pentatonic scale. We learned 1 octave in open position.

We learned 2 licks in G Major, building blocks to a bigger vocabulary.

We practice and play with backing tracks to put it in a real time context and real world situation as close as you can get to playing with people.

CHAPTER 2

TUNE IN

"I am a musician and a guitar player. Music is my language and my guitar is my voice. Music is Melody, Harmony and Rhythm. I develop my language skills and my instrument skills. They are two separate worlds working together to complete the circle of music."

Rhythm is the number one factor to sounding great as a musician.

WARM UP

Muted String Ladder(MSL) 2 strings Quarter-notes 60 BPM

Muted String Ladder(MSL) 2 strings Eighth-notes (2 per string) 60 BPM

SHELLS

SHELL PRINCPAL:

Whatever fingering you choose
play it **THE SAME WAY** *ascending* and *descending*.
Then <u>**REVERSE**</u> the **order of the fingers**
and **play it THE SAME WAY** in both directions.

SHELL 0 2   Quarter-notes (not written) and 8ths (as written)   60 BPM

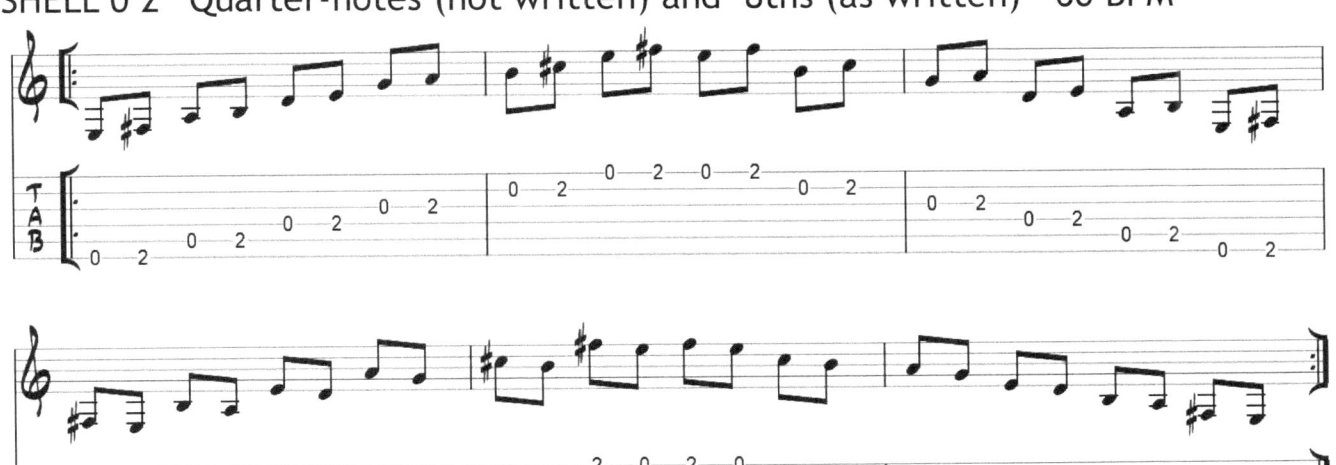

SHELL 0 3   Quarter-notes   60 BPM

Lead Guitar Level 1   CHAPTER 2

EXERCISE

G Major Pentatonic scale 1 octave   Quarter-notes   60 BPM

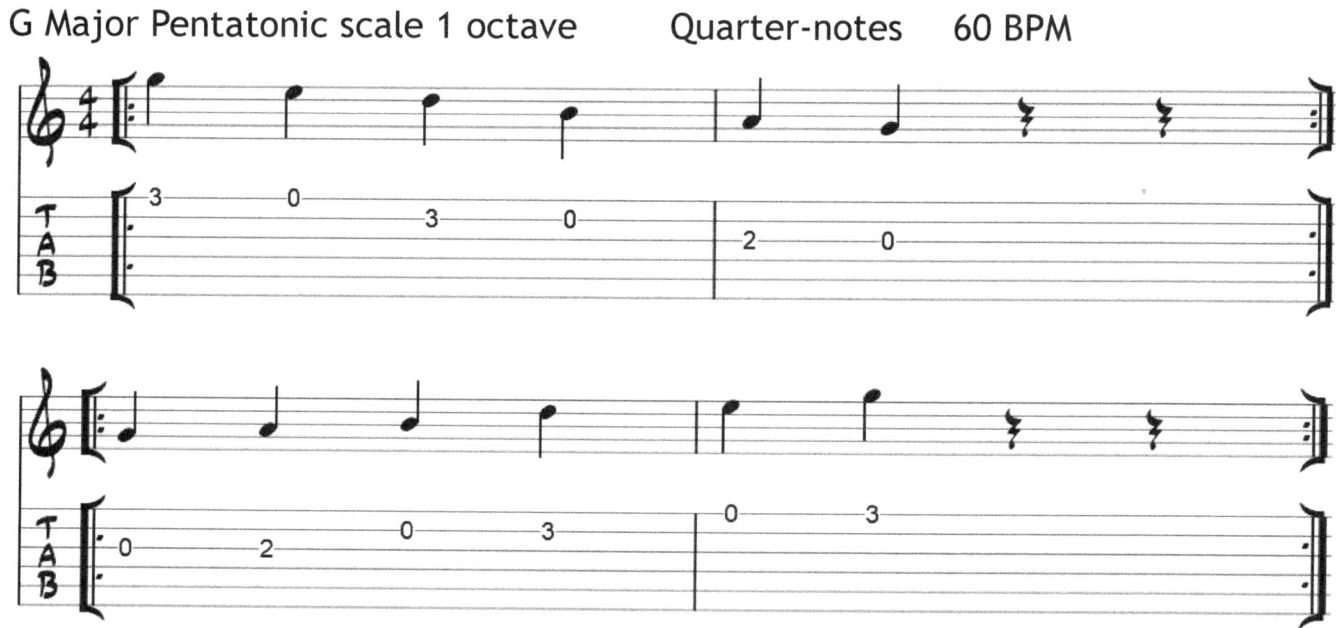

G Major Pentatonic scale 1 octave   Eighth-notes   60 BPM

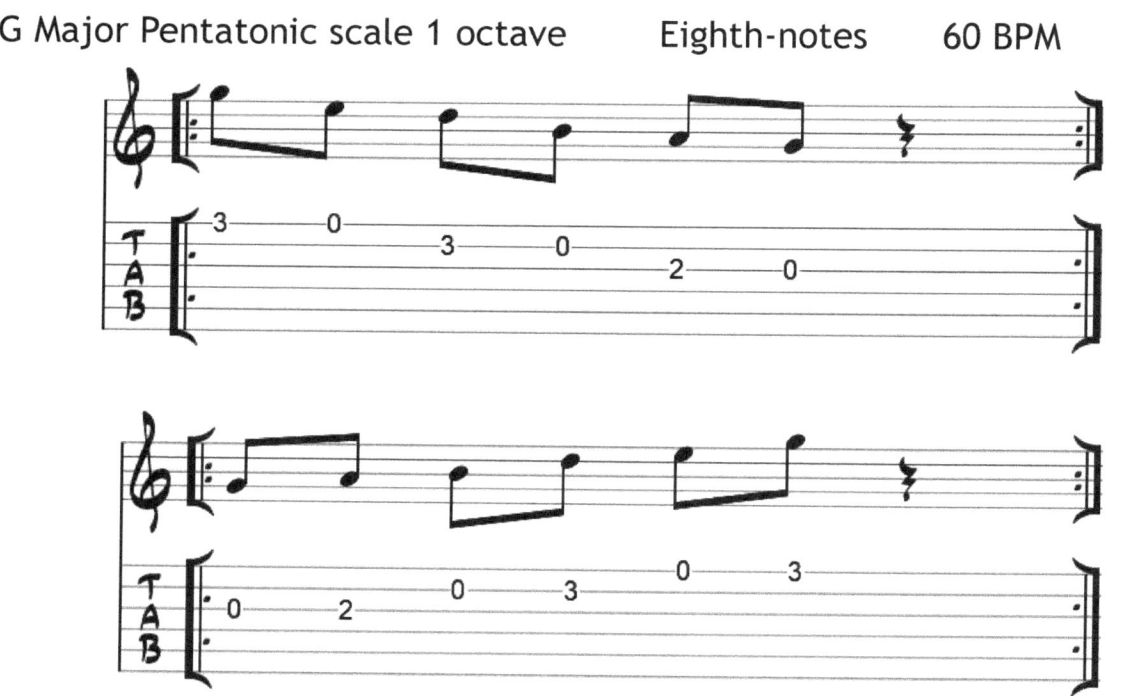

REVIEW

G Major Lick #1 Quarter-notes and Eighth-notes

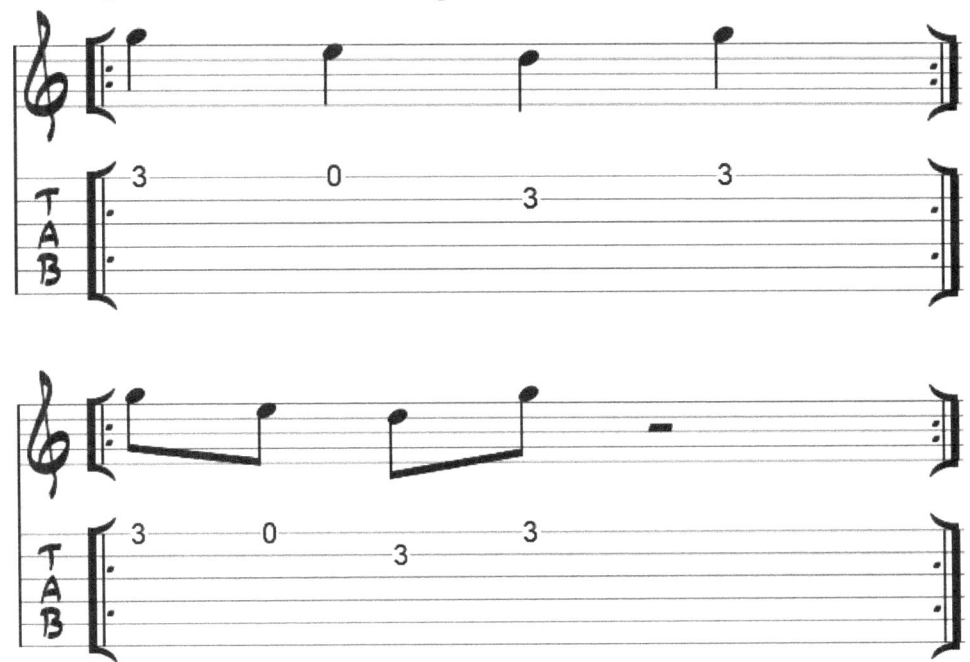

G Major Lick #2 Quarter-notes and Eighth-notes

PENTATONIC SCALES

As we mentioned in Chapter 1 Pentatonic scales are ancient scales that are in all styles of music all over the planet. They are ingrained in human beings. They are vocal melodies (for example Amazing Grace), guitar solos, riffs, and bass lines. They are everywhere in music.

There are two main types of pentatonic scales, Major and minor.

Major pentatonic scales have an upbeat happy innocence to them, but they can also be very soulful and endearing. They go with Major chords/progressions.

Minor pentatonic scales have a more solemn and blues feel and are very evocative. They go with minor chords/progressions.

Below is a 1 octave E minor pentatonic scale: **E G A B D**

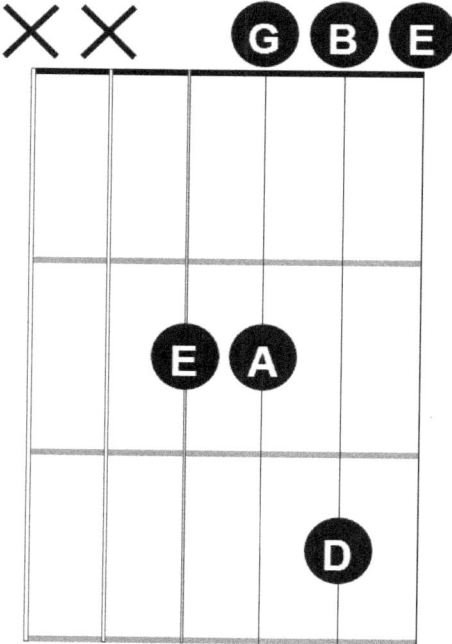

***You will notice the notes are the same for an E minor Pentatonic as the G Major Pentatonic. This is a very special relationship called *Relative Major-relative minor.* We will go deeper into this topic in the next chapters.

PRACTICE

E minor Pentatonic scale Descending 1 octave   Quarter-notes   60 BPM

E minor Pentatonic scale Descending 1 octave   Eighth-notes   60 BPM

E minor Pentatonic scale Ascending 1 octave   Quarter-notes   60 BPM

E minor Pentatonic scale Ascending 1 octave   Eighth-notes   60 BPM

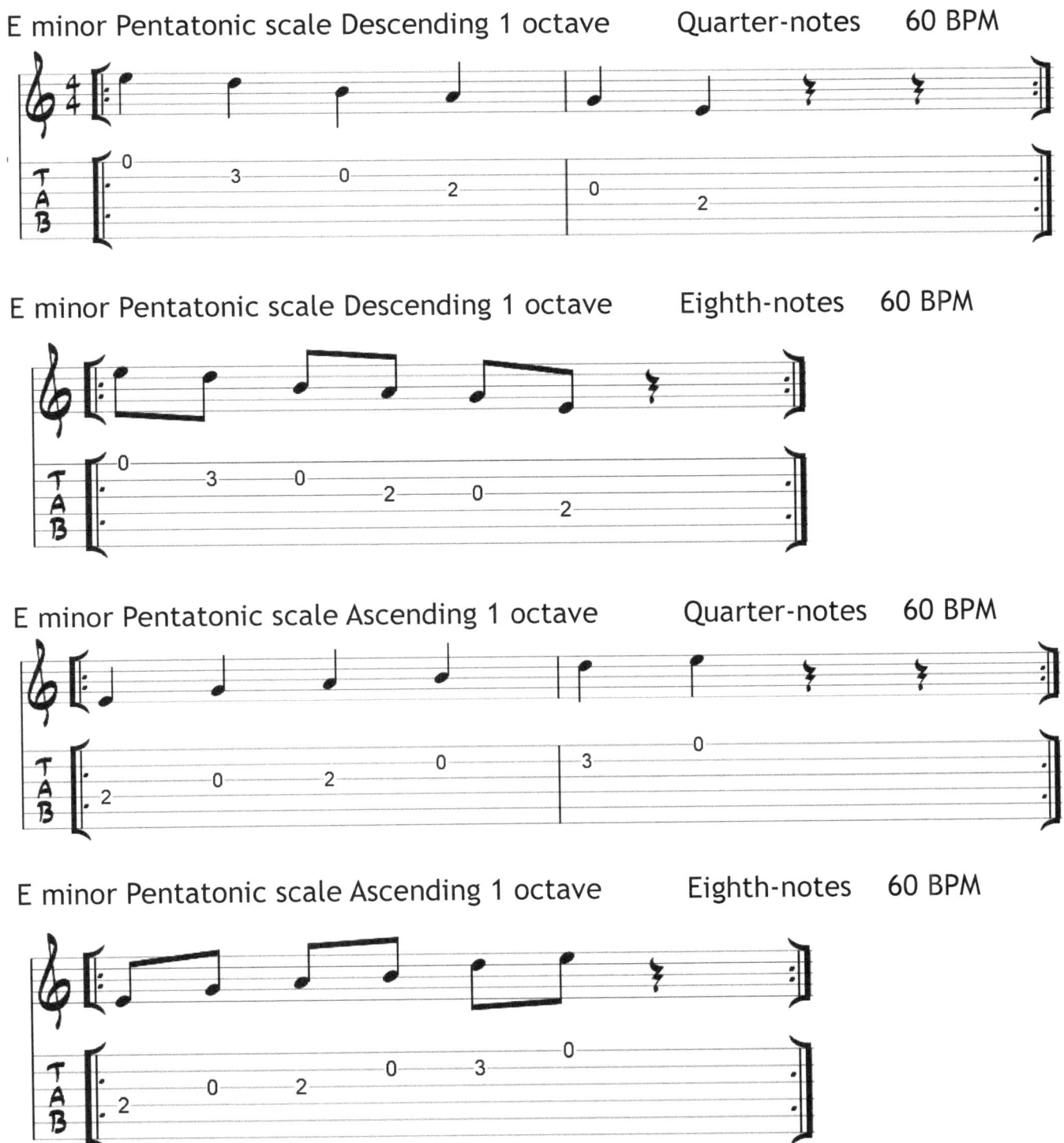

HOW TO CHOOSE A SCALE

We make our music decisions first and then go to our instrument.

First we need to know the chords of our song, or of the section of the song we are going to solo over.

Then we decide which chord is the "Main" chord. (The "main" chord is not necessarily the Key we are in, although it often is the same). We need to find which one of these chords sounds like "home." (Which chord does it come to rest on? Which chord would you end on if you were playing it at a concert.

Strum the chord progression below a few times and you will realize that the Em chord is the "Main" chord.

Now as a MUSICIAN we match a E minor Chord with a E minor Pentatonic scale. This is global. The scale for the main chord should work for all the chords. This is playing globally.

As a Guitar player we know a 1 octave E minor pentatonic scale in the open position.

$\frac{4}{4}$|Em |D |Am |C   ‖

For the follow-along BACKING TRACK VIDEO visit

www.LeadGuitarWorkshop.com

LICKS

E minor Lick #1 Quarter-notes and Eighth-notes
*** The 3rd fret on the high E string is a G note (which is in the scale, higher than our root E)*

E minor Lick #2 Quarter-notes and Eighth-notes

BACKING TRACKS

Backing Tracks are one of the best ways to practice lead guitar. First, they are a time keeper. There is a drum beat and a groove. They also have chords, which are necessary for scales to sound properly. Chords provide a harmonic backdrop to give context and color to the melody notes (solo). You can practice the scales over backing tracks, and you can play licks over the backing tracks and eventually solo.

BACKING TRACK #1

$\frac{4}{4}$ |G |D |Em |C ||

Use a G Major pentatonic scale for practice.
Use the 2 G Major pentatonic LICKS to start to solo.

BACKING TRACK #2

$\frac{4}{4}$ |Em |D |Am |C ||

Use a E minor pentatonic scale for practice.
Use the 2 E minor pentatonic LICKS to start to solo.

SUMMARY

We are musicians.
We are guitar players.
We learn the language of music.
We learn the craft of playing the guitar as an instrument.

We warm up with Muted String Ladders (MSL) and SHELLS.

We EXERCISE our scales ascending and descending with quarter-notes and eighth-notes.

We learn musical ideas (LICKS) to start to build "musical conversation."

We use BACKING TRACKS to give a real time context to our playing.

We will learn the incredible power of the relationship between the Relative Major and minor in solos and songs (very important).

CHAPTER 3

TUNE IN

"I am a musician and a guitar player. Music is my language and my guitar is my voice. Music is Melody, Harmony and Rhythm. I develop my language skills and my instrument skills. They are two separate worlds working together to complete the circle of music."

Rhythm is the number one factor to sounding great as a musician.

WARM UP

MSL 3 string   Quarter-notes   60-70 BPM

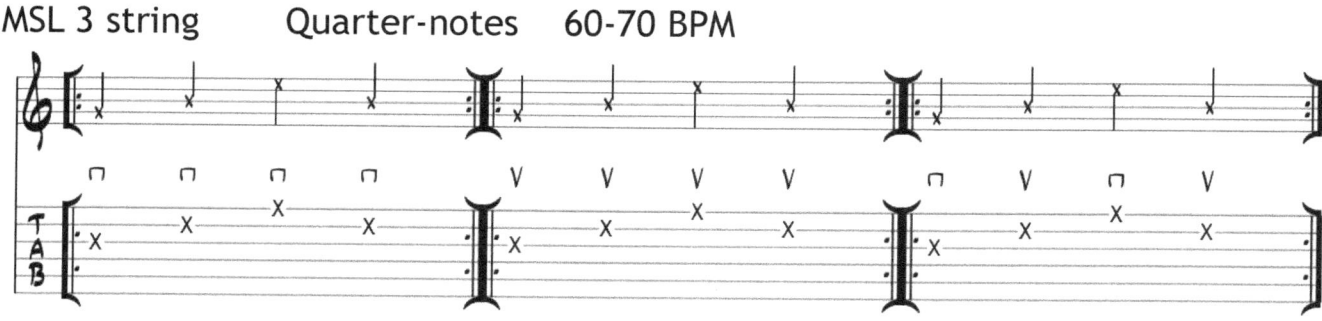

MSL 3 string   Eighth-notes   60-70 BPM

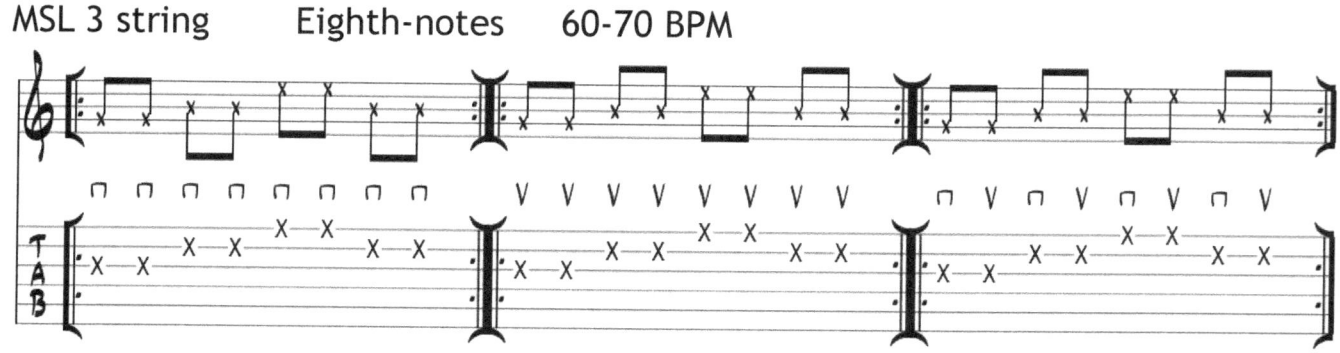

SHELL 0 2   Eighth-notes 60-70 BPM

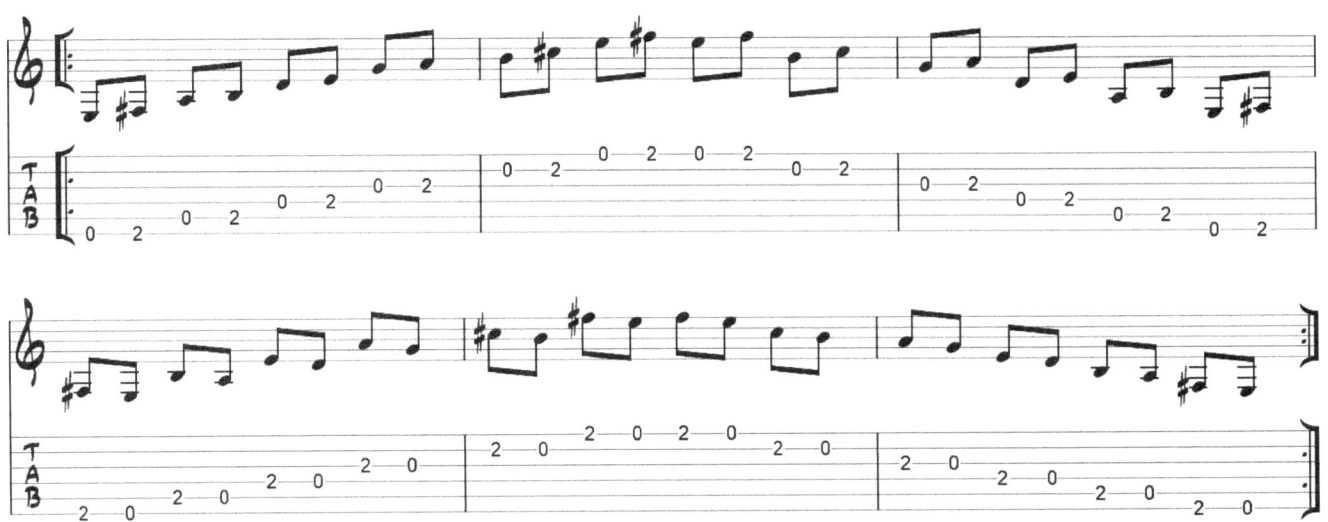

SHELL 0 3   Eighth-notes 60-70 BPM

EXERCISE

1 Octave G Major pentatonic scale   Eighth-notes   60 BPM

1 Octave E minor pentatonic scale   Eighth-notes   60 BPM

G Major Licks #1 and #2   Eighth-notes   60 BPM

E minor Licks #1 and #2   Eighth-notes   60 BPM

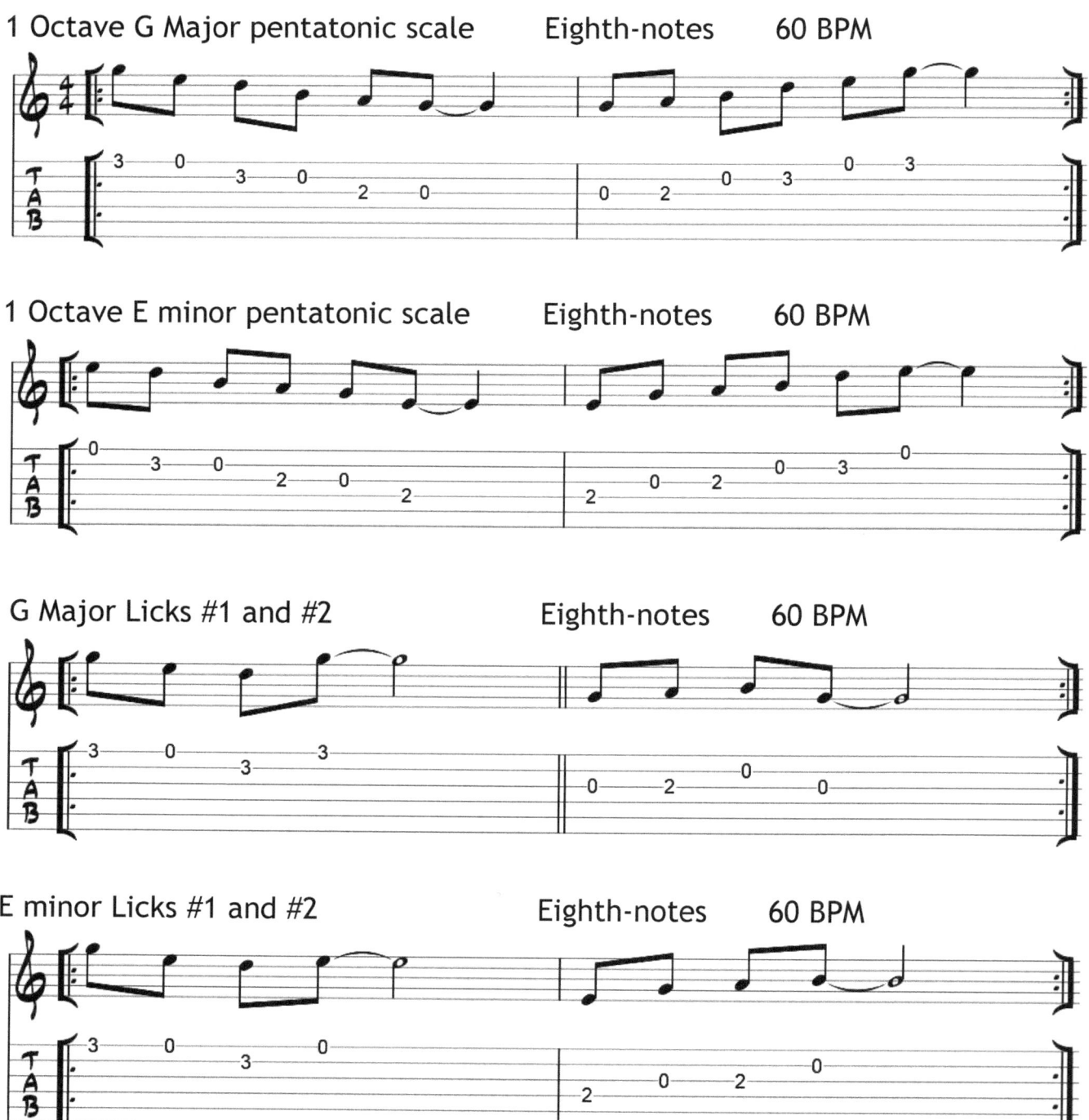

**The last note is TIED to the previous note. Looking at the TAB it looks the same but with the tie, the note sustains for the duration of the tied note. Some are quarter-notes and the hollow notes are HALF-NOTES (2 beats).

RELATIVE MAJOR AND RELATIVE MINOR

As a musician we need to understand that for every Major Key there is a relative minor key. They have the same notes and the same chords, but they start on different notes. I like to think of this as a house. It has a front door and a back door. Each door looks and feels different but they are both entries into the same house with the same family inside.

The two scales we have looked at, G Major and E minor pentatonic, are relatives. They share the same notes and come from the same key in which they share the chords.

The **G Major pentatonic scale** is: **G A B D E**
The **E minor pentatonic scale** is: **E G A B D**

They are the same notes and they contain the notes of both chords.

G Major chord: G B D
E minor chord: E G B

The relationship of relative Major and relative minor is one of the most fundamental and beneficial things to know in music, it doubles your knowledge. This relationship happens 12 times in music, one for each note.

The 12 **Keys** have relatives. (Key of G Major *IS* the key of E minor, same notes and chords, different root)
The 12 **chords** have relatives. (G and Em chords)
The 12 **scales** have relatives. (G and E minor pentatonic scales)

Relative chords are often swapped out for one another in songs. They also create sections of the song. For example the verse of the song could be in E minor and the chorus in G Major (Relative Major). Neil Young does this in "Rockin' in the Free World."

Relative Major and Relative minor relationship is what I call a "**Musical Truth.**". It is one of the many common things in the language of music that all musicians know despite what instrument they play.

PENTATONIC SCALE 2 OCTAVES

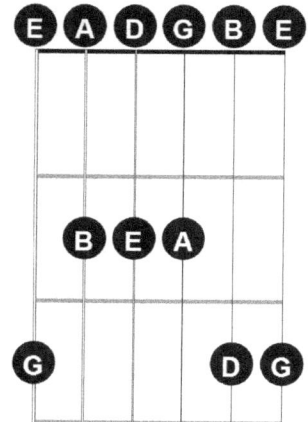

Pattern #1 as Quarter-notes and Eighth-notes

ROOT NOTE LOCATIONS for Pattern #1

G Major Pentatonic

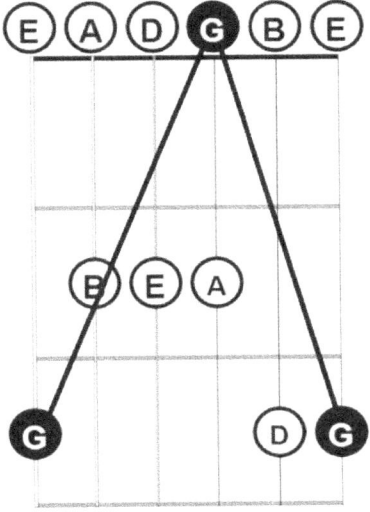

E minor pentatonic

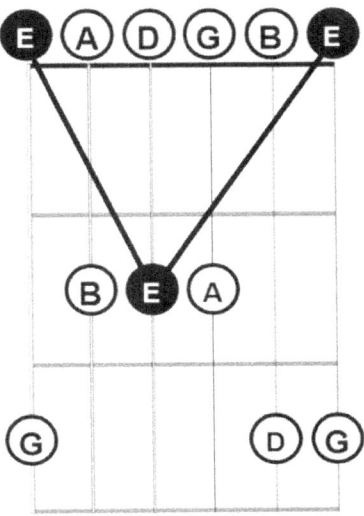

When comparing the G Major to the E minor pentatonic scales, the location of the roots make V shapes in the opposite directions. This relationship is really important as it stays true for any note on any fret on the fretboard.

Since the pentatonic scale contains both G Major and E minor chords, you can see how the open chords are part of the notes in the scale.

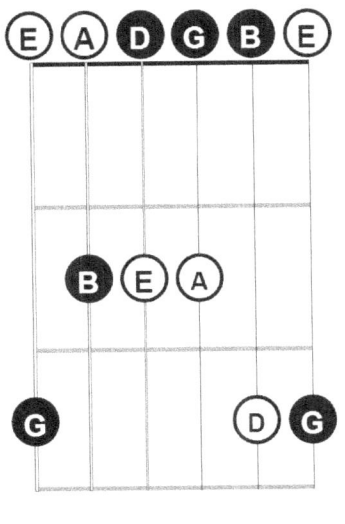

G Major chord

E minor chord

LICKS

G Major Lick 1   Octave lower   Quarter and Eighth-notes

G Major Lick 2   Octave lower   Quarter and Eighth-notes

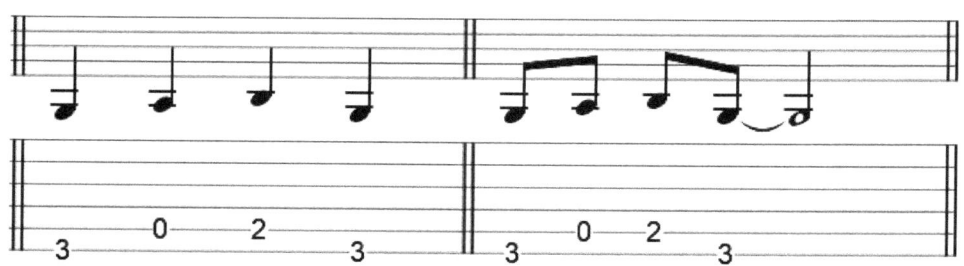

E minor Lick 1   Octave lower   Quarter and Eighth-notes

E minor Lick 2   Octave lower   Quarter and Eighth-notes

SUMMARY

We are musicians.
We are guitar players.
We learn the language of music.
We learn the craft of playing the guitar as an instrument.

We warm up with Muted String Ladders (MSL) and SHELLS.

We EXERCISE our scales ascending and descending with quarter-notes and eighth-notes

We learn musical ideas (LICKS) to start to build "musical conversation."

We use BACKING TRACKS to give a real time context to our playing.

We will learn the incredible power of the relationship between the Relative Major and relative minor in solos and songs (very important).

CHAPTER 4

TUNE IN

"I am a musician and a guitar player. Music is my language and my guitar is my voice. Music is Melody, Harmony and Rhythm. I develop my language skills and my instrument skills. They are two separate worlds working together to complete the circle of music."

Rhythm is the number one factor to sounding great as a musician.

WARM UP

Muted String Ladder (MSL) 6 string Quarter-notes   60 BPM

Note the bar of 2/4 time in the 3rd bar. It is there to keep an even back and forth across the six strings. It keeps a steady flow. It needs ten beats to start the cycle over again. It could also have been written as two bars of 5/4.

Muted String Ladder (MSL) 6 string   Eighth-notes   60 BPM

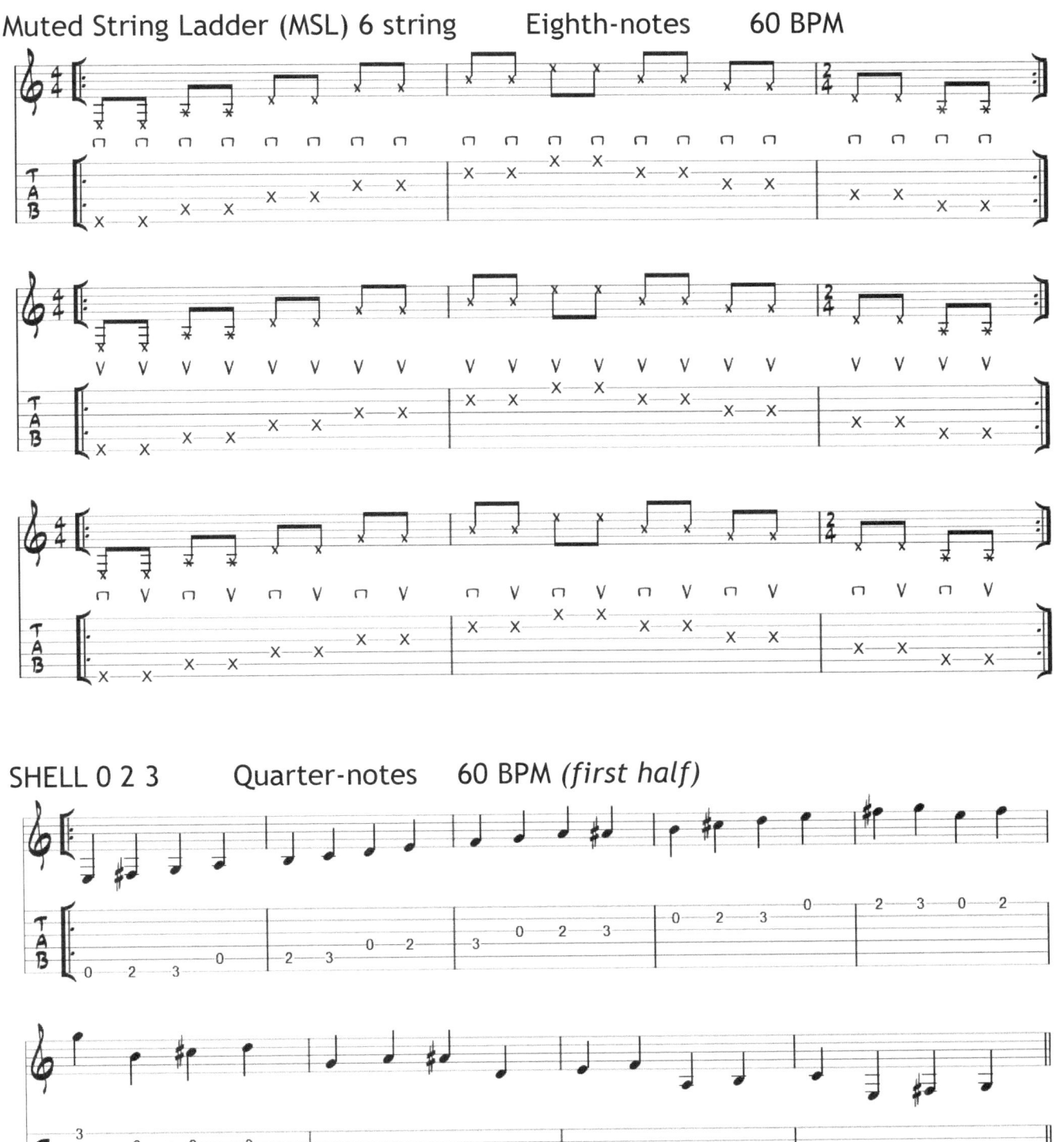

SHELL 0 2 3   Quarter-notes   60 BPM *(first half)*

SHELL 0 2 3   Quarter-notes   60 BPM *(second half)*

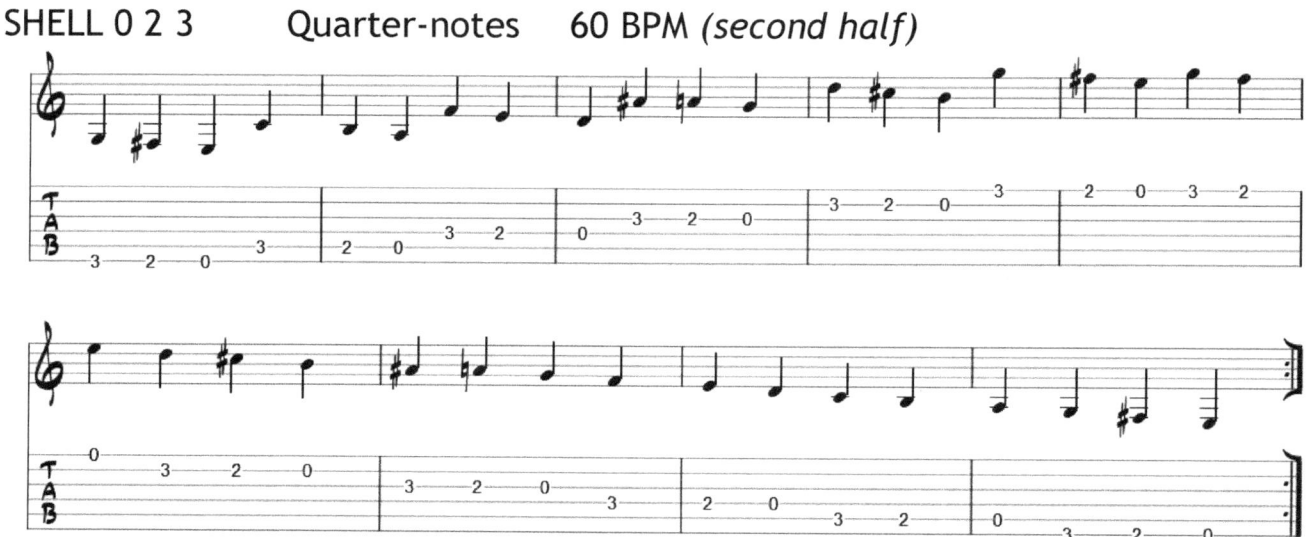

EXERCISE

Pattern #1 Pentatonic Scale in Quarter-notes and Eighth-notes

REVIEW

The Relative Major/relative minor relationship is one of the best things to know as a musician. You will see it and use it all the time. It's occurring in Keys chords and scales. It will help you figure out and remember songs, and you will use it for soloing (melodies) too.

Every scale needs a chord to help it do its job. Scales can work fine on their own, but when played with a chord they take on the color of the chord because the chord has a root note too and that puts the scale in perspective.

The root of the scale sounds like a note at rest. The other notes in the scale add tension (in a good way). Music is a game of tension and resolution.

As a musician we need to know where the root is to help resolve phrases and give breath. As guitar players we see them in our patterns.

Roots move in Relatives. So do intervals and this is why one sounds Major and one sounds minor.

As a guitar player Pattern #1 is very powerful. The first two notes of the scale are the Relatives in the key (G and Em). This helps us to easily remember the musical relationship.

Also keep in mind that pattern #1 is a two octave shape. (Low E string to High E string is two octaves, 24 piano keys apart.) The guitar as an instrument is about 3 usable octaves and a 4th in the key of E. This means that pattern #1 covers 2/3rds of the range of your instrument.

LEGATO Hammer-ons and Pull-offs

Legato is a term used for when a musician connects the notes of a phrase with a smooth and consistent sound without any silence in between the notes. Each instrument offers different ways to achieve this. Wind instruments play many notes with one breath instead of tonguing each note. String players play many notes with one bowing. Piano players let each note overlap as they change notes. As guitar players we have a few choices. We have Hammer-ons and Pull-offs, slides, and bends.

Legato is illustrated with a curved line over the *different notes*. It's important to understand that legato is different from a *rhythmic tie* which connects the *same notes*.

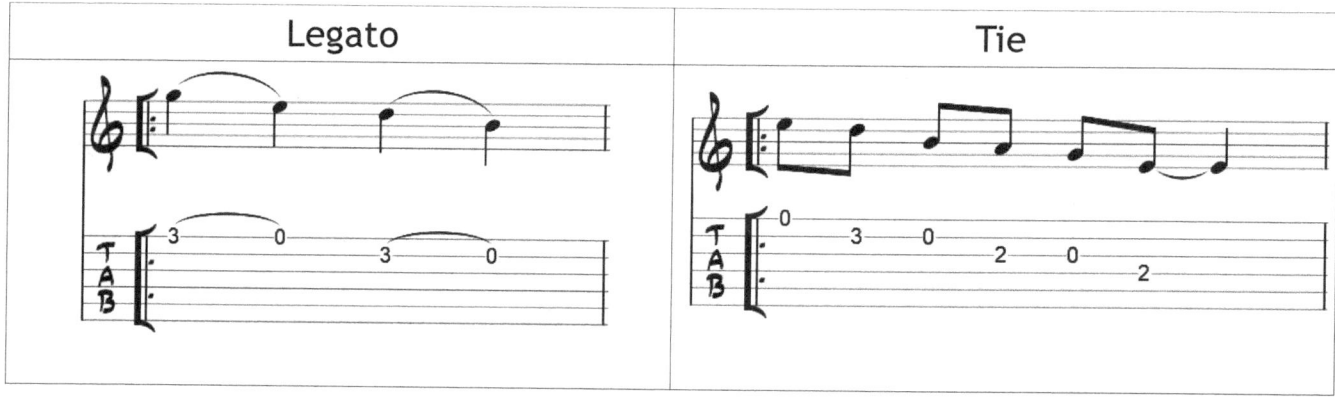

As a guitar player hammer-ons and pull-offs (HO, PO) are complimentary as they each do half of the job.
Hammer-ons are for ascending notes and pull-offs are for descending notes.

Watch video at www.LeadGuitarWorkshop.com

PRACTICE

Pattern #1 as Pull-offs (PO)   Quarter-notes   60 BPM

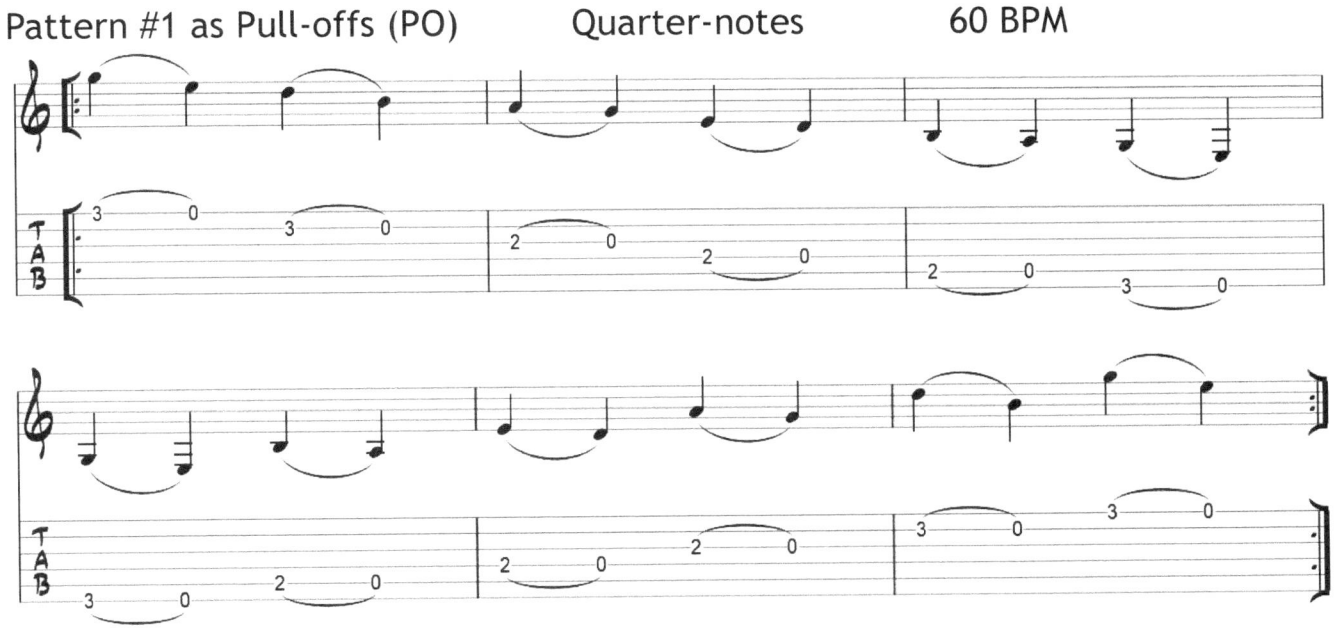

Pattern #1 as Hammer-ons (HO)   Quarter-notes   60 BPM

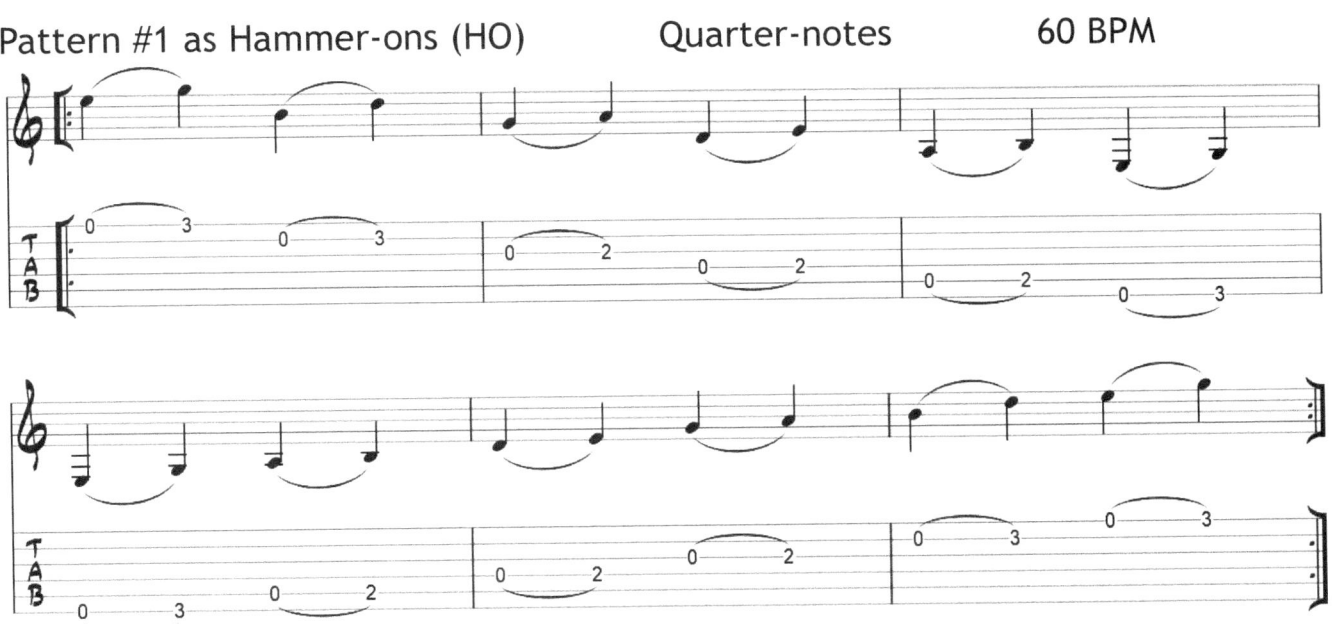

LICKS with HO PO

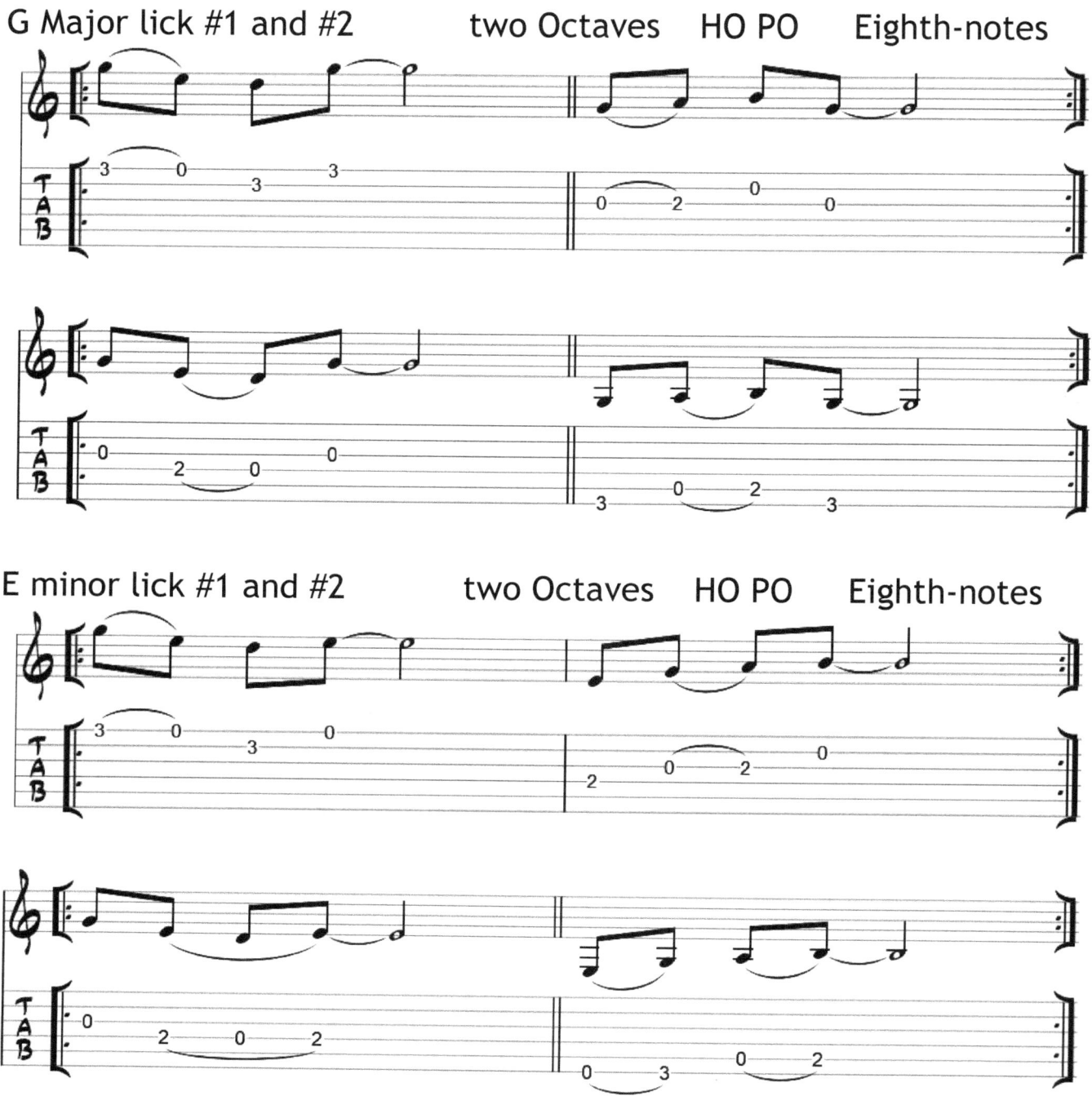

REMEMBER: A rhythmic tie is different than a legato symbol (HO PO). Although they look the same, the tie is a sustained note and legato is the sound of the consistent transition from one note to the next note.

SUMMARY

We are musicians.
We are guitar players.
We learn the language of music.
We learn the craft of playing the guitar as an instrument.

We warm up with Muted String Ladders (MSL) and SHELLS.

RHYTHM is most important.

We EXERCISE our scales ascending and descending with quarter-notes and eighth-notes

We learn musical ideas (LICKS) to start to build "musical conversation."

We learned what Legato is as a MUSICIAN and how to use it as a GUITAR PLAYER with HAMMER-ONS and PULL-OFF'S.

It is essential to remember that Rhythm still happens when you are playing in a legato style. So often students play HO or PO super quickly when they don't need to. You must follow the original melodic idea. The legato ENHANCES the idea, it DOES NOT CHANGE the idea.

We use BACKING TRACKS to give a real time context to our playing.

We will learn the incredible power of the relationship between the Relative Major and relative minor in solos and songs (very important).

CHAPTER 5

TUNE IN

"I am a musician and a guitar player. Music is my language and my guitar is my voice. Music is Melody, Harmony and Rhythm. I develop my language skills and my instrument skills. They are two separate worlds working together to complete the circle of music."

Rhythm is the number one factor to sounding great as a musician.

WARM UP

MSL 6 Strings Quarter-note *(not written)* and 8th's *(written)* 60-80 BPM

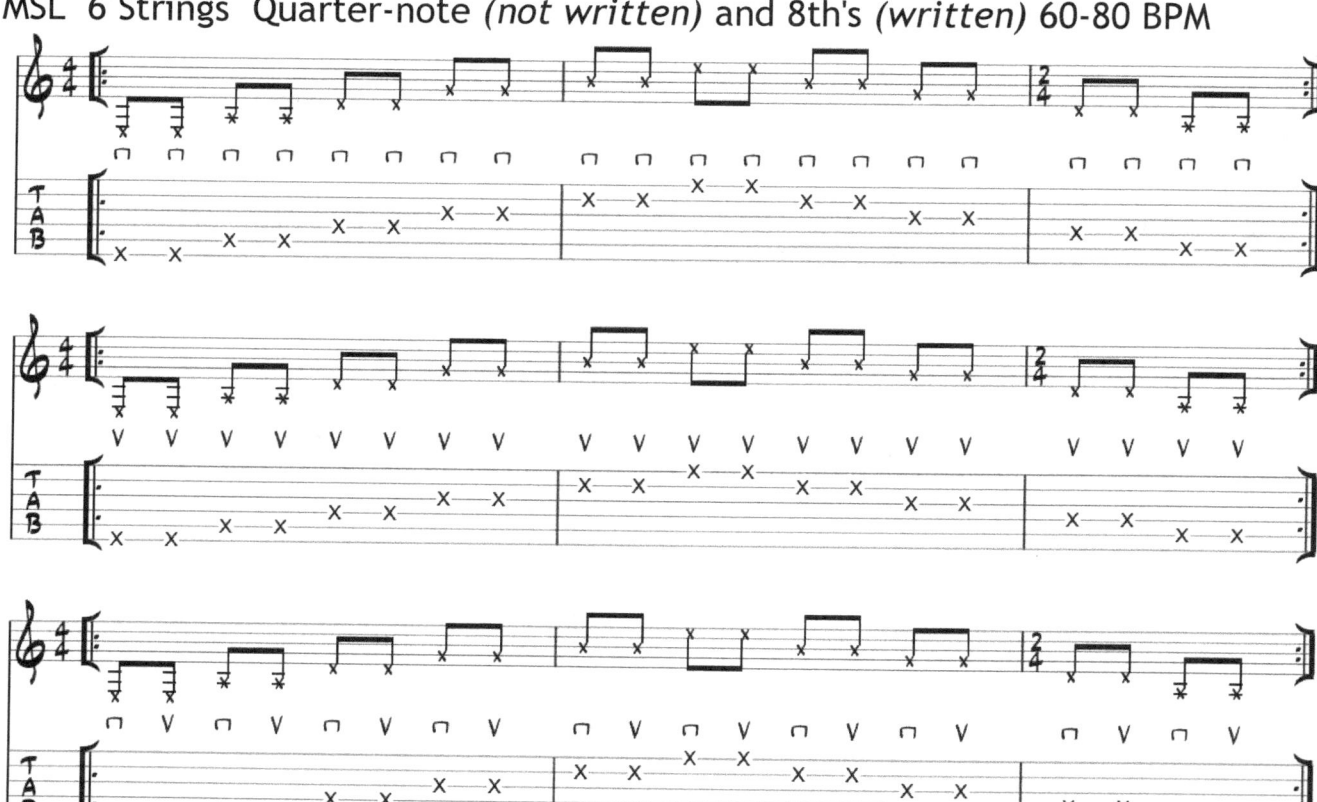

SHELL 0 2   HO PO   Quarter notes

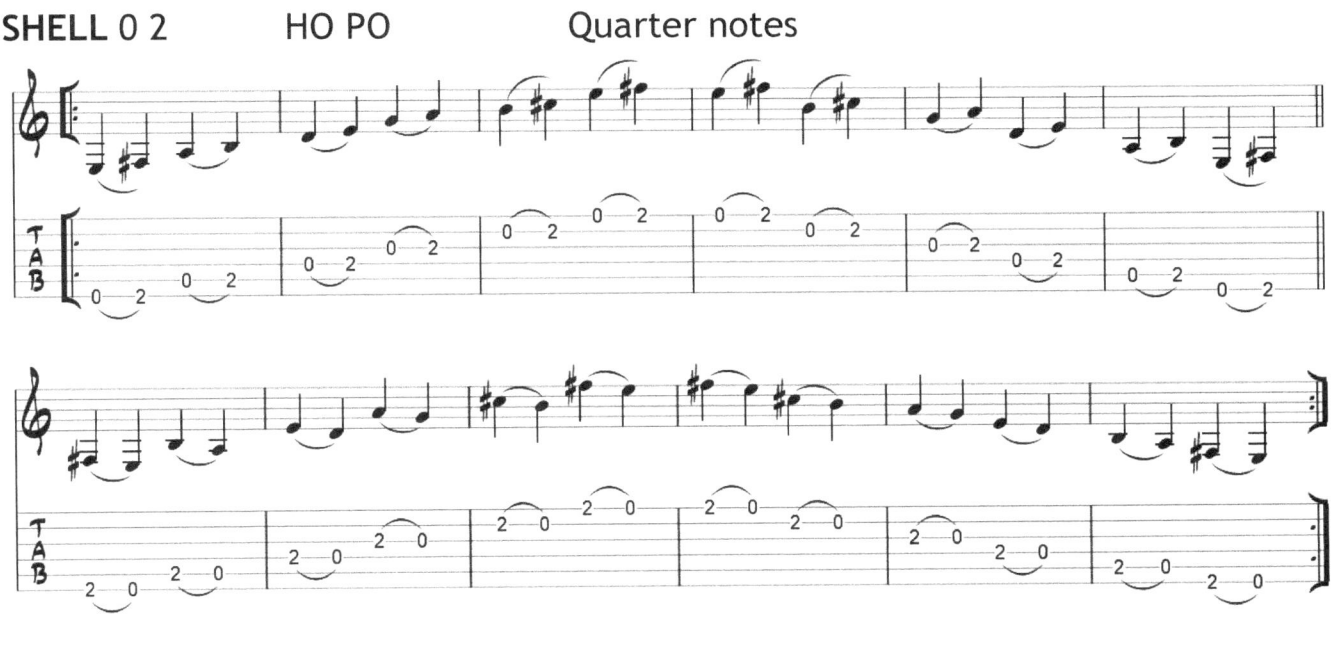

SHELL 0 3   HO PO   Quarter-notes

EXERCISE

Pattern #1   Quarter-notes   60-80 BPM

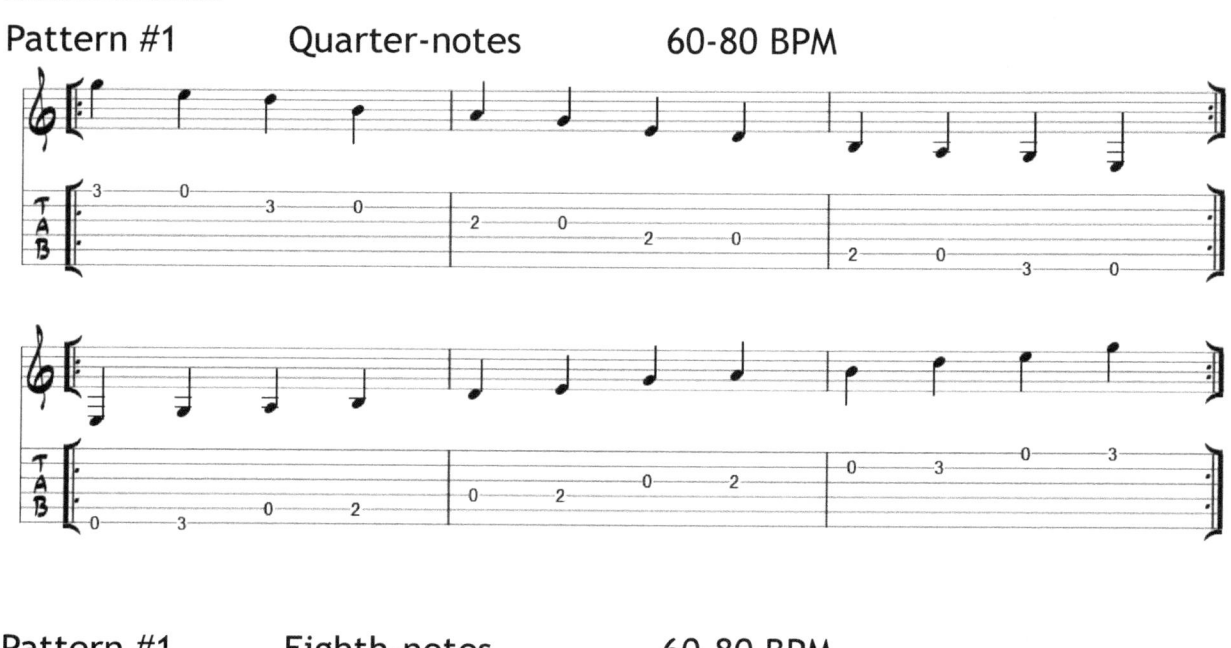

Pattern #1   Eighth-notes   60-80 BPM

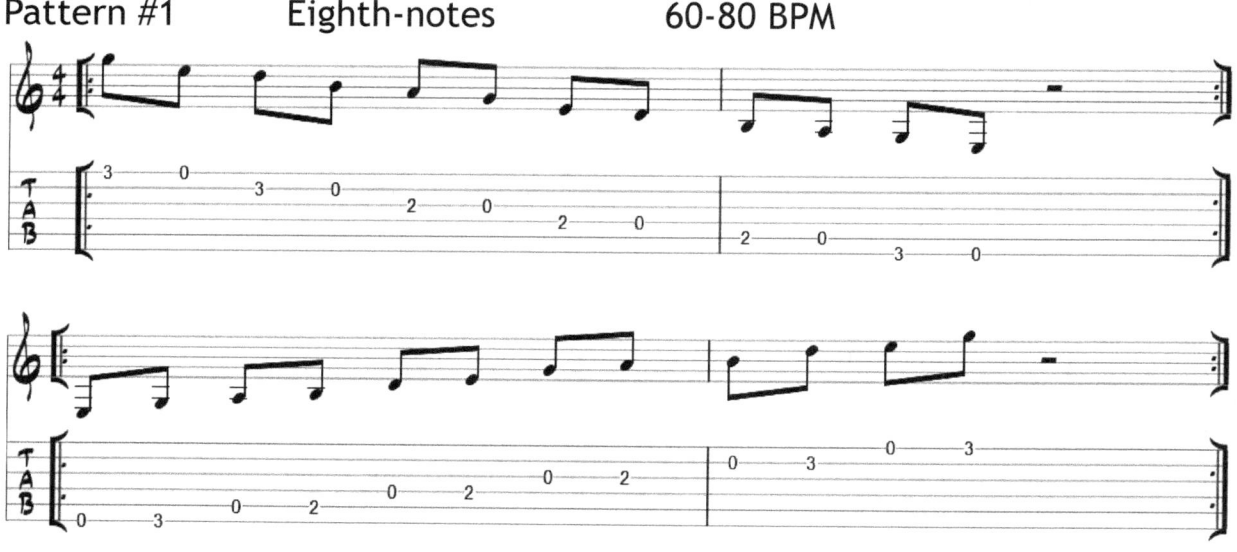

Pattern #1 PO   Quarter-notes   60 BPM

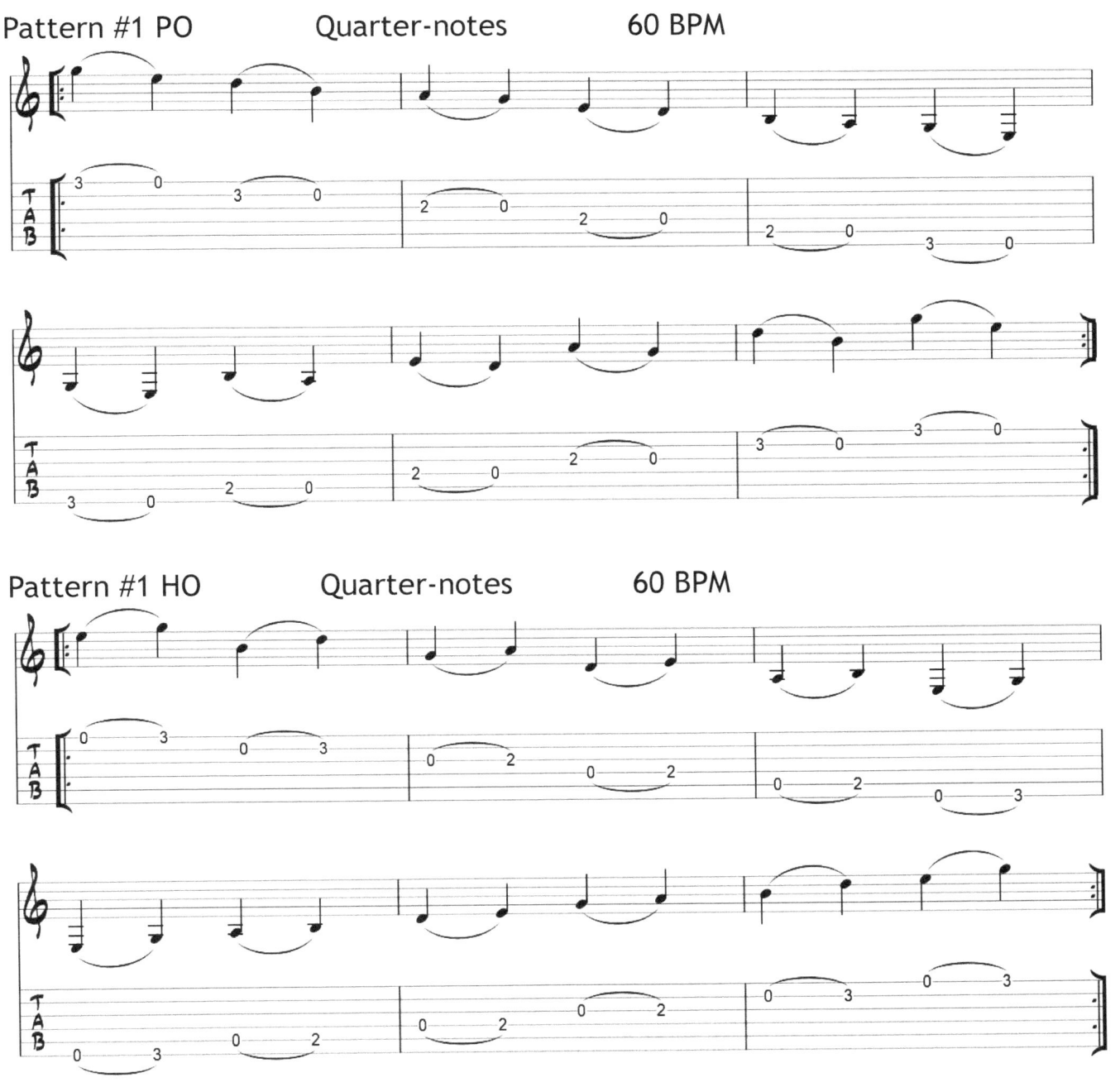

REVIEW

G Major lick #1 and #2   two Octaves   HO PO   Eighth-notes

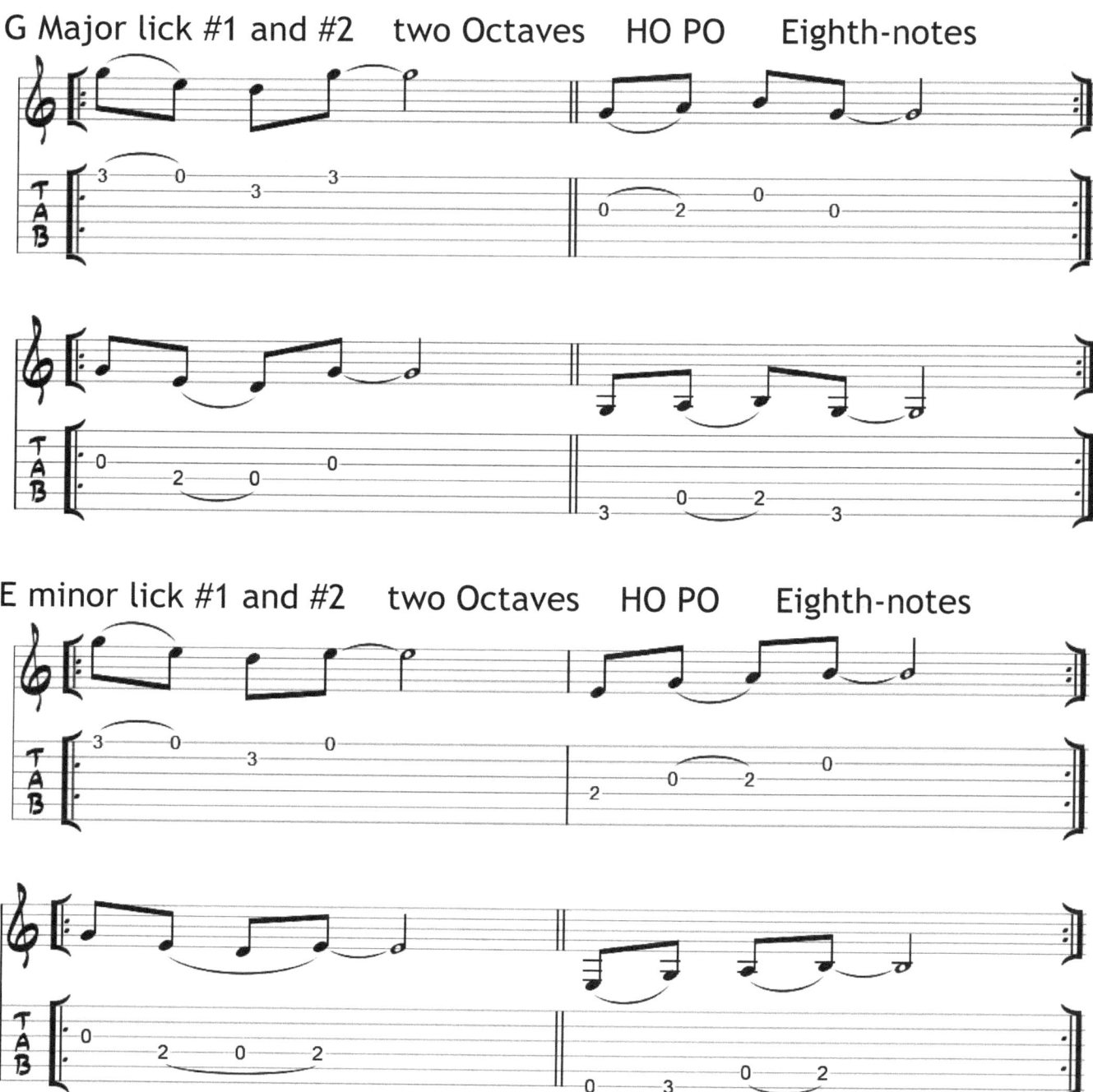

E minor lick #1 and #2   two Octaves   HO PO   Eighth-notes

REMEMBER: A rhythmic tie is different than a legato symbol (HO PO). Although they look the same, the tie is a sustained note and legato is the sound of the transition of the note. ALSO, the two octaves look and feel very different even though they are the SAME NOTES.

KING BOX

The "King Box" is a slang term I heard Stevie Ray Vaughn call the upper part of pattern #2. In the big picture there are 5 total pentatonic shapes (traditional) that encompass the 12 frets for a key. We have looked at Pattern #1 and the King Box is the top 3 strings of Pattern #2. For guitar payers this little spot is like your neighborhood, a comfy and familiar area to do a lot of cool things. Guitar players love to hang out in this spot. I often say that you can make a career out of Pattern #1 and the King Box. Most of what Jimi Hendrix and Stevie Ray Vaughn did utilized this knowledge (as well as countless others).

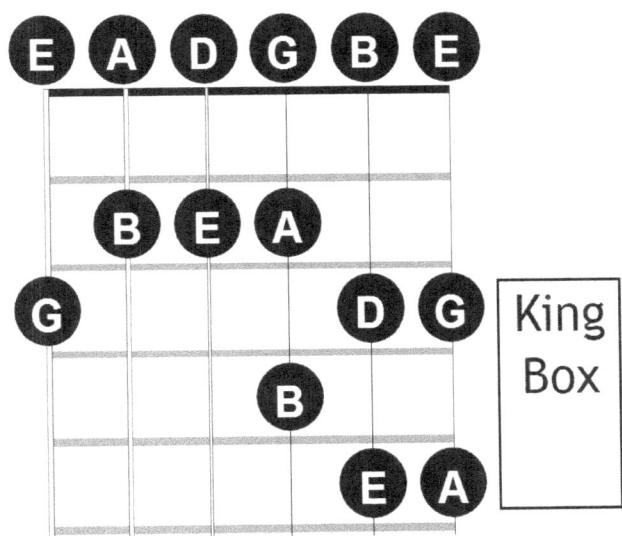

All of our music ideas are the same and unchanged. This is still the same 5 note pentatonic scale we have been using (G Major and E minor). BUT, as a guitar player this further allows access to the same notes higher up on our guitar. This adds more control over notes and the ability to do HO PO without open strings and slides.

To watch the VIDEO visit
www.LeadGuitarWorkshop.com

King box as Quarter-notes

King Box as Eighth-notes

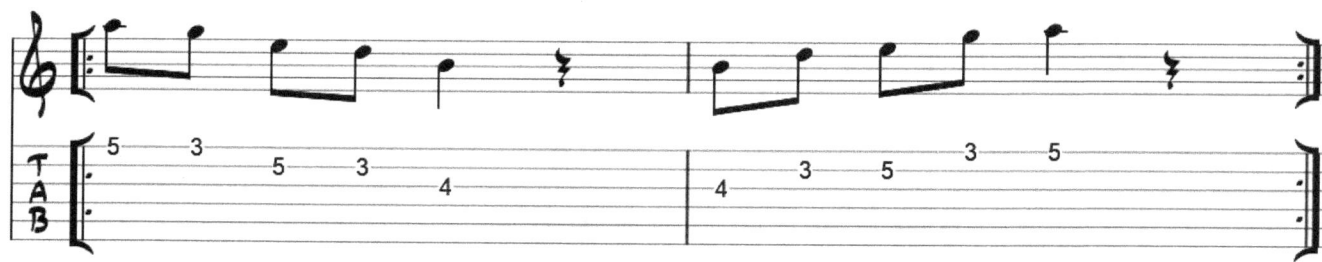

SLIDES

Slides are another tool for guitar players to achieve a **legato** sound. You can slide any finger on any one string up or down, and on up to all six strings (for example sliding a bar chord). Slides are shown with the Legato arch as well as a straight/angled line to tell you it is a slide. Squeeze hard enough to make sure the note is sounding as you pass over the frets, but don't squeeze so hard as to restrict your fretboard hand from moving up and down the neck as you slide.

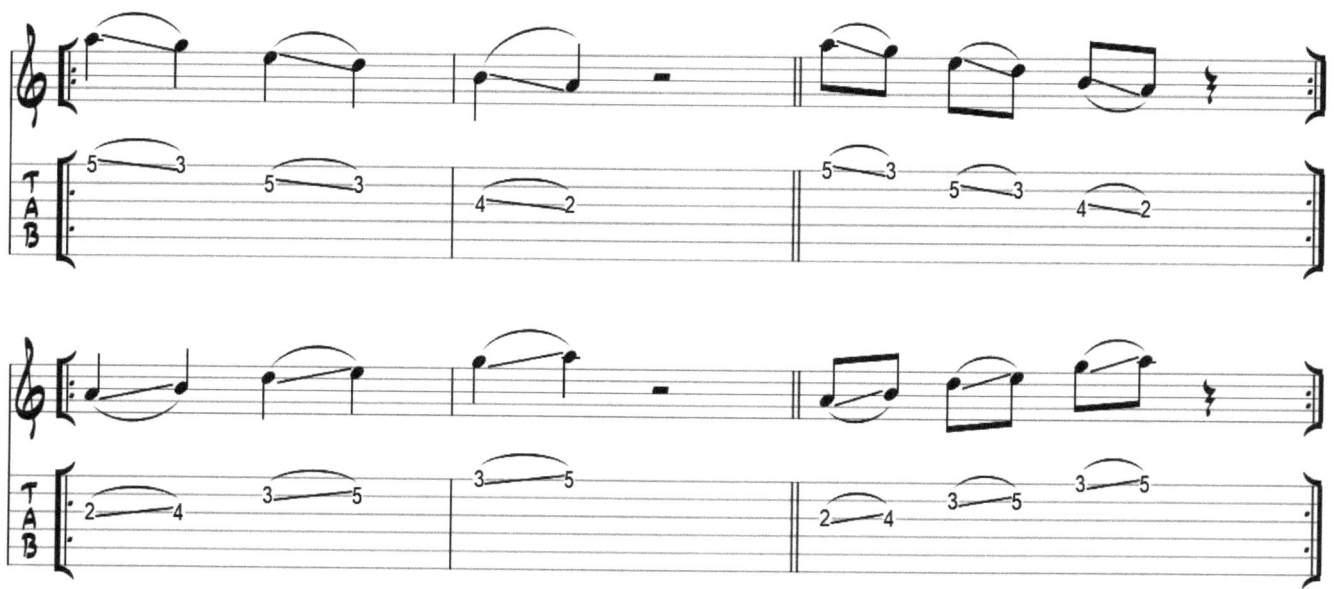

PRACTICE

Lick #1 G Major played in the King box   Quarter-notes and Eighth-notes

Lick #1 E minor played in the King box   Quarter-notes and Eighth-notes

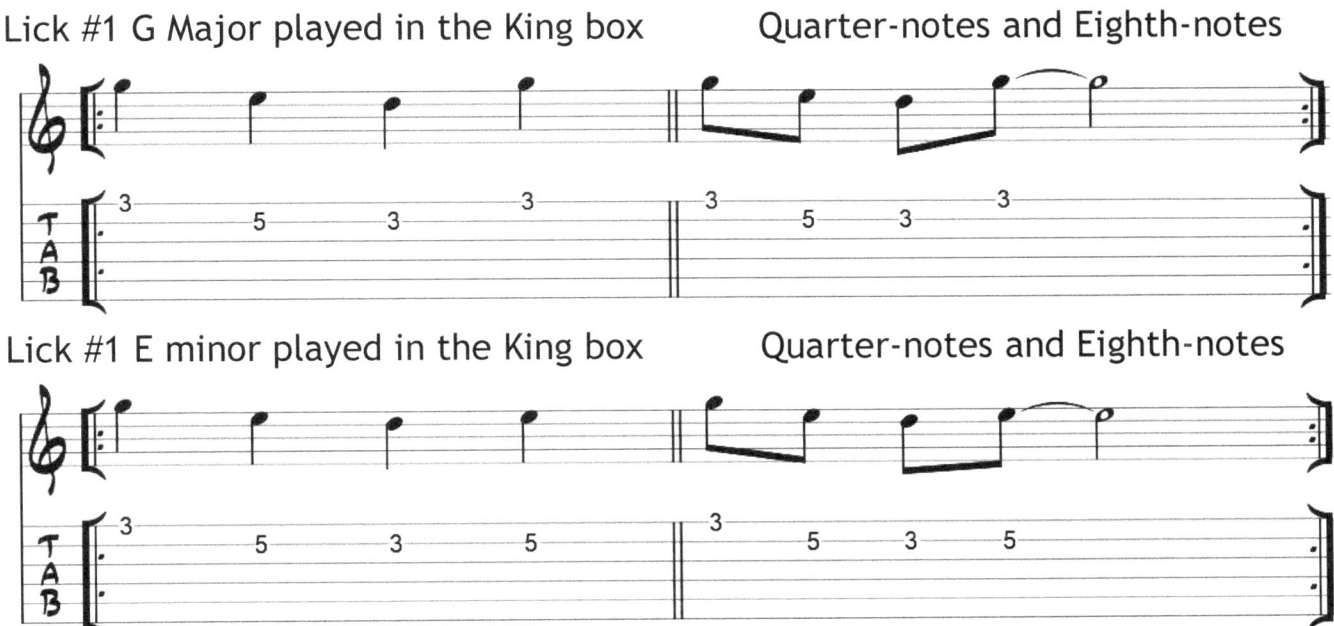

LICK 1-2 Slide Lick

Without a doubt, one of the coolest an most popular ways to go from Pattern #1 into the King Box is to slide on the G string. This lick has thousands of variations and different ways that players "dress this up." I refer to it as the "1-2 Slide lick." Every guitar player uses this move in some way.

1-2 Slide Lick G Major   Quarter-notes and Eighth-notes

1-2 Slide Lick E minor   Quarter-notes and Eighth-notes

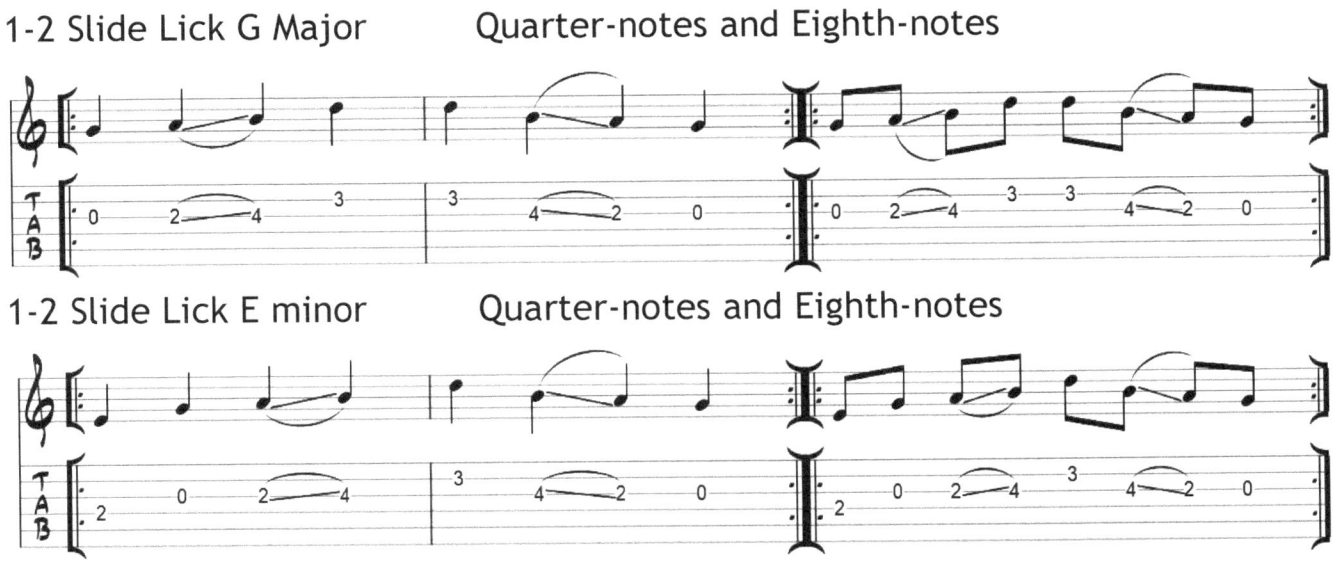

SUMMARY

We are musicians.
We are guitar players.
We learn the language of music.
We learn the craft of playing the guitar as an instrument.

We warm up with Muted String Ladders (MSL) and SHELLS.

RHYTHM is most important.

We EXERCISE our scales ascending and descending with quarter-notes and eighth-notes.

We learn musical ideas (LICKS) to start to build "musical conversation."
A lick is NOT a static snapshot of an idea. It is flexible, malleable, able to be pushed and pulled with different inflections and rhythms, and different combinations of the notes. Licks have an endless tweak-ability.

We learned what Legato is as a MUSICIAN and how to use it as a GUITAR PLAYER with HAMMER-ONS, PULL-OFF'S and SLIDES.

We added the King Box to extend the range of our scale.

It is essential to remember that Rhythm still happens when you are playing in a legato style. So often students play HO or PO super quickly when they don't need to. You must follow the original melodic idea. The legato ENHANCES the idea, it DOES NOT CHANGE the idea.

We use BACKING TRACKS to give a real time context to our playing.

As musicians we learn to see and use the Relative Major and relative minor relationship.

CHAPTER 6

TUNE IN

"I am a musician and a guitar player. Music is my language and my guitar is my voice. Music is Melody, Harmony and Rhythm. I develop my language skills and my instrument skills. They are two separate worlds working together to complete the circle of music."

Rhythm is the number one factor to sounding great as a musician.

WARM UP

MSL 6 strings   Quarter-notes and Eighth-notes   60-80 BPM *(not written)*

MSL 1 string   Quarters/Eighths/Triplets 60 BPM (count 1-trip-let, 2-trip-let)

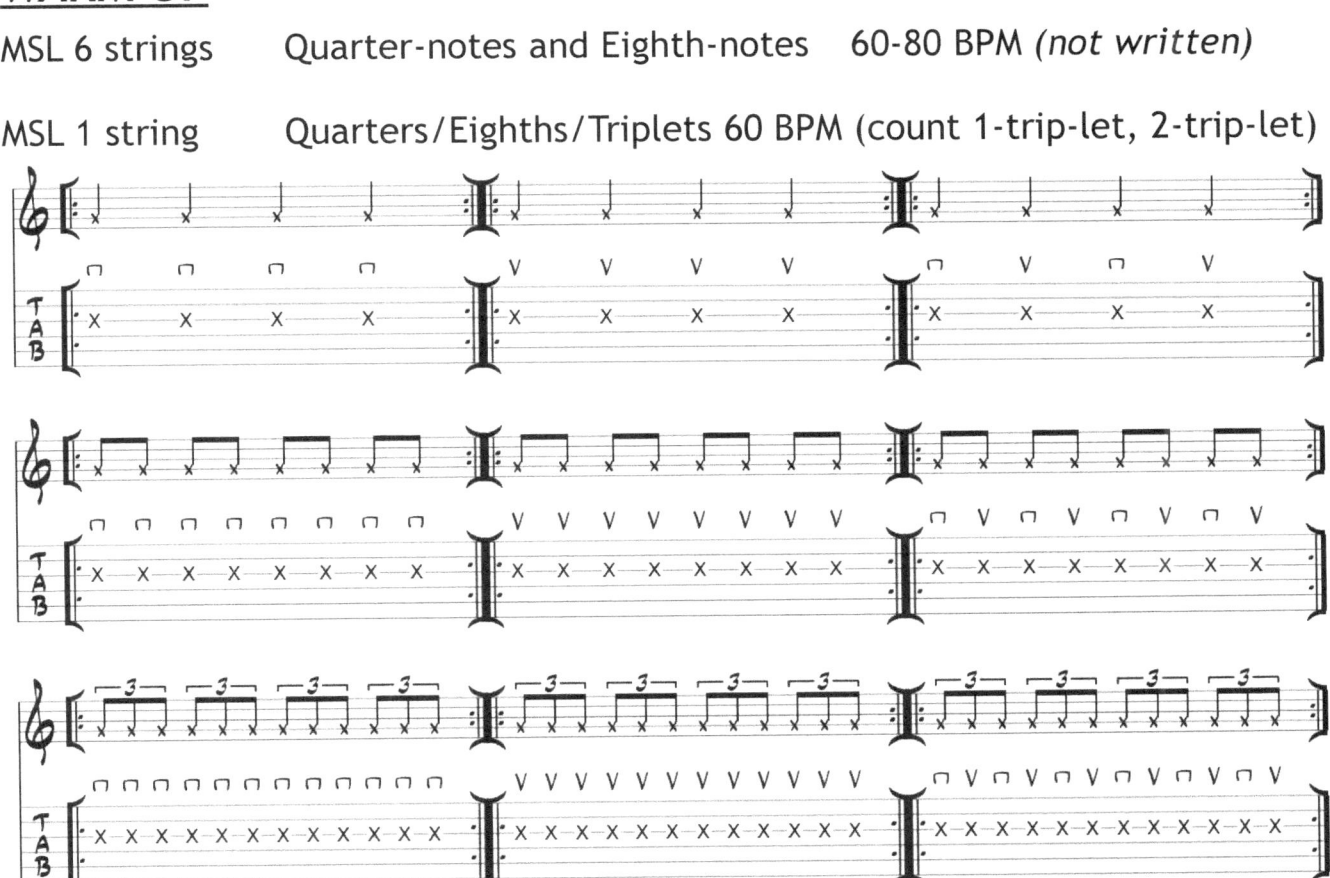

It's really import to understand and feel how alternate picking flip flops every other beat in triplets. It's DOWN-UP-DOWN on the first beat and then UP-DOWN-UP for the second beat, and then it repeats.

SHELL 0 1 2 3   Quarter-notes   60 BPM

SHELL 1 3   Quarter-notes   60 BPM

EXERCISE

Lick #1 G Major played in the King box   Quarter-notes and Eighth-notes

Lick #1 E minor played in the King box   Quarter-notes and Eighth-notes

1-2 Slide Lick G Major   Quarter-notes and Eighth-notes

1-2 Slide Lick E minor   Quarter-notes and Eighth-notes

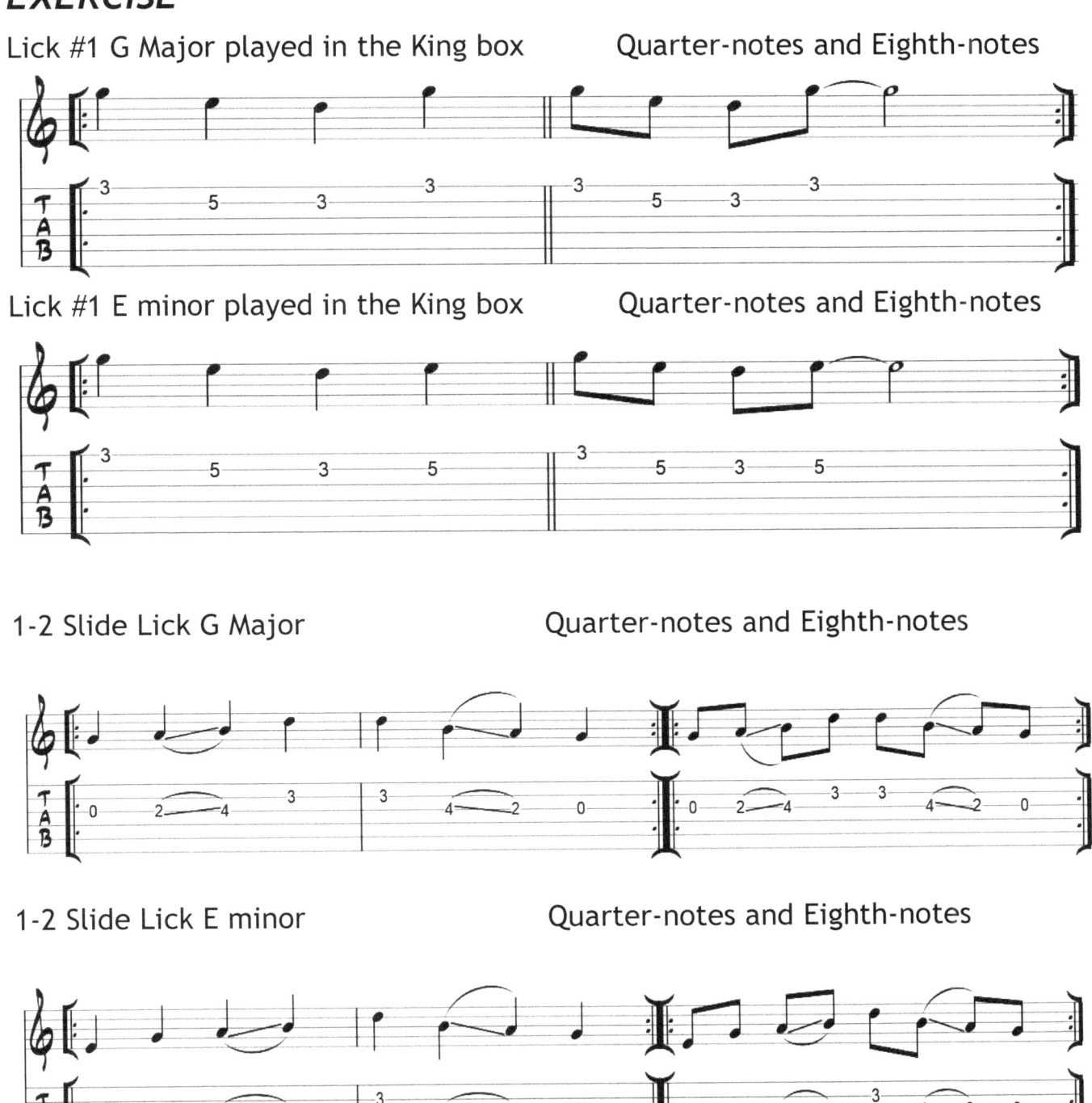

SELF GENERATING

One of the best ways to "practice" is not to practice, but to play! So far we have been using backing tracks which are as close to playing with a band as you can get without the band.

Self-generating music is a term I use when a musician just "turns on" the song in their inner ear; can generate a beat enough to start playing and plays a chord and then a solo/riff. Usually it's one bar back and forth but it can be two or more bars or even split measures. ALWAYS KEEP TIME. Start at 60 BPM.

ONE Bar RHYTHM-One bar SOLO

TWO Bar RHYTHM-TWO Bar SOLO

SPLIT MEASURE-2 Beats RHYTHM-2 Beats SOLO

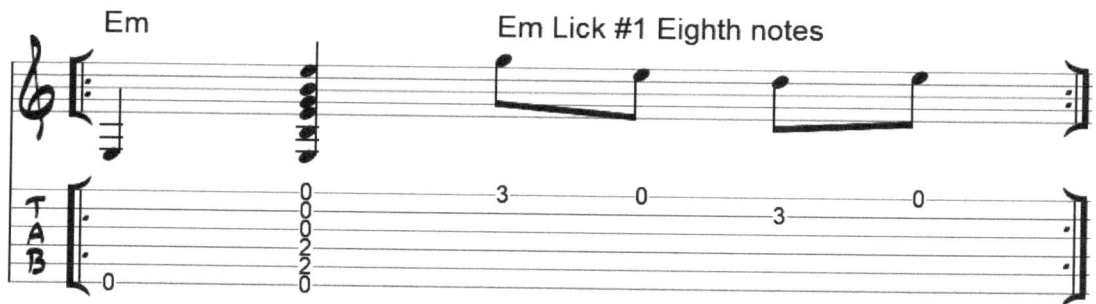

You can always vary the rhythm part and change up the licks. You must keep time. Use a metronome at first to keep you solid and accountable to the beat. Often metronomes allow you to change the sound of the first beat.

REVIEW

We should always think and ask our music questions first before we go to the instrument. We look at our chord progression and figure out which chord is the "main" chord and then base our scale decision on that chord. Scale matches the chord. If the main chord is A then the scale would be A Major pentatonic. If the main chord is B minor, then use a B minor pentatonic.

The relationship of relative Major and relative minor is one of the most fundamental and beneficial things to know in music. It doubles your knowledge. This relationship happens 12 times in music, one for each note.

The 12 **Keys** have relatives. (key of G Major *IS* the key of E minor, same notes and chords, different root.)
The 12 **chords** have relatives. (G and Em chords)
the 12 **scales** have relatives. (G and E minor pentatonic)

Relative chords are often swapped out for one another in songs. They also create sections of the song. For example the verse of the song could be in E minor and the chorus in G Major (Relative Major). Neil Young does this in "Rockin' in the Free World."

Relative Major and Relative minor relationship is what I call a **"Musical Truth."** It is one of the many common things in the language of music that all musicians know despite what instrument they play.

As a guitar player we have learned a two octave, open position pattern for an E minor and G Major pentatonic. These are relatives and share the same notes.

This particular pattern only works for G Major and E minor when in the open position. If we need any of the other Major and minor pentatonics (to go with chords other than G and Em) we need to move Pattern #1 to its proper note/fret and it will be a closed pattern (no open strings). This is just like an open E minor chord. To move it we have to make a BAR to move it to the other 11 keys. We will do the same with Pattern #1.

NOTES ON THE E STRING

As a guitarist we need to know the names of the notes on our outer strings (the E strings). Not only do we navigate bar chords this way but we will also navigate the pentatonic scales this way.

As a musician we know the Musical Truth that **EF and BC are half-steps** and have no fret in between. This is true of open strings too. It's easier to first see the Natural notes (no sharps (#) or flats (b)). Aside from the EF and BC relationship, all the other notes have a whole-step between them (1 fret in between). Keep in mind that you know the notes of the open strings, so you will also know them across the 12th fret, an octave higher.

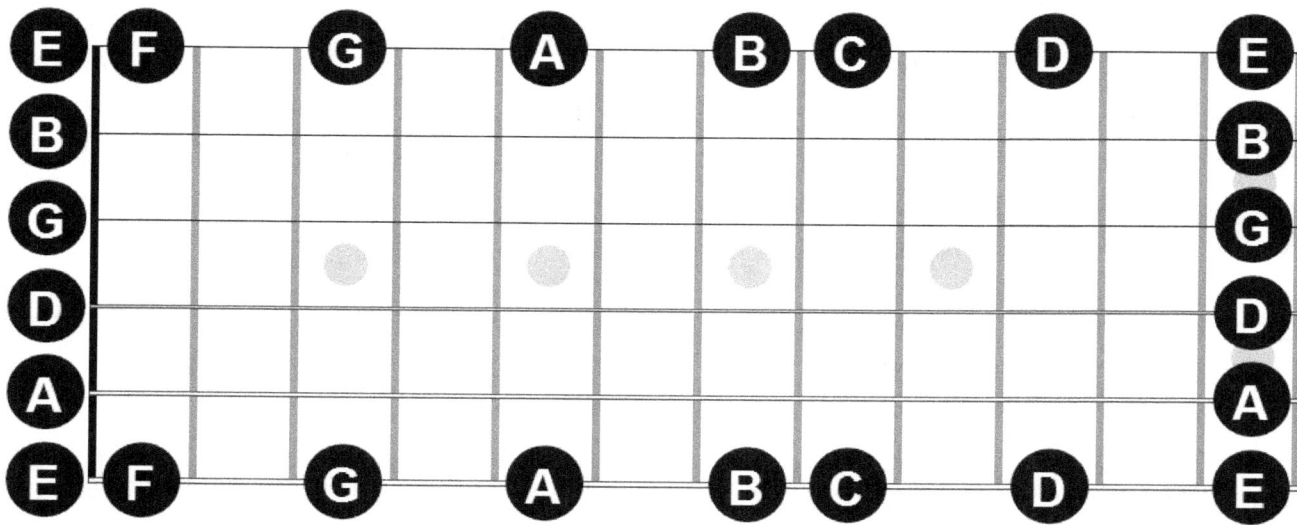

ROCK AND ROLL RULE

One of the the greatest things I ever learned on guitar is what I call the "Rock and Roll Rule." It is a quick and easy way to see how **PATTERN #1** connects the two notes that are RELATIVES. The first two notes of pattern #1 point to the Relative Major and Relative minor. The first finger (the lower sounding note) is the relative minor and the pinky (the higher sounding note) is the relative Major.

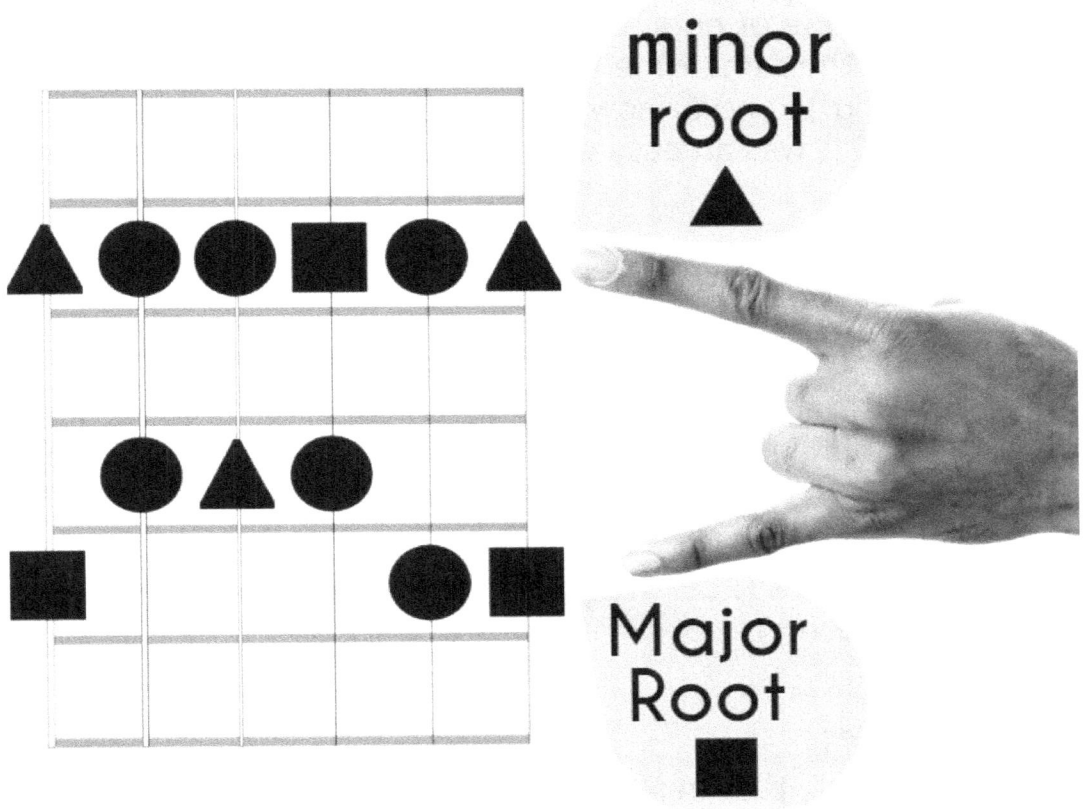

PATTERN #1 Rock and Roll Rule

PRACTICE

On the high E string, start with quarter-notes at 60 BPM. Starting with E note, go up the Natural notes and name each one as you go by. Stop on the 12th fret. Repeat that note and descend the string back to E, the open string.

TIP: When I was young I had a diagram of the notes of the neck and I didn't know what I was looking at. I had just learned the G chord and noticed that there was a G note on the 3rd fret. I figured thats why the G chord was named G. I also noticed this was on the first DOT of my fret board (3rd fret). I decided to check the next couple of dots, and they were the notes A and B. I said "GAB" out loud. (At the same time I realized my mom was "gabbing" on the phone with her friend.) Forever now to be known as GAB are the first 3 dots (usually) on a guitar. It was an easy way to see the notes on the E string.

HOW TO FIND A SCALE

1. Pick chord. (for example A Major)
2. Find the ROOT note on the E string. (A=5th fret)
3. Decide if the scale is Major or minor (depending on chord) and place either the FIRST finger or the PINKY. (pinky for A Major)
4. Lay down PATTERN #1. (2nd fret to 5th fret for A Major)(BONUS: it also is F# minor pentatonic)

NAVIGATE PATTERN #1
Find the ROOT, the fret, the finger to match the chord. What is the RELATIVE?

1. A Major
2. A minor
3. D Major
4. E Major
5. D minor
6. B minor
7. G minor
8. F# minor
9. Bb Major

SUMMARY

We are musicians.
We are guitar players.
We learn the language of music. Melody, Harmony, and Rhythm.
We learn the craft of playing the guitar as an instrument.

We warm up with Muted String Ladders (MSL) and SHELLS.

RHYTHM is most important.

We EXERCISE our scales and licks.

We learn musical ideas (LICKS) to start to build "musical conversation."
A lick is NOT a static snapshot of an idea. It is flexible, malleable, able to be pushed and pulled with different inflections and rhythms, and different combinations of the notes. Licks have endless tweak-ability.

We learned what Legato is as a MUSICIAN and how to use it as a GUITAR PLAYER with HAMMER-ONS, PULL-OFFS, and SLIDES.

As a guitar player we added the King Box to extend the range of the scale.

We use BACKING TRACKS and SELF GENERATE to give a real time context to our playing.

We use PATTERN #1 Rock and Roll Rule to navigate our scales and to easily see the relationship between the Relative Major and Relative minor.

You will use Pattern #1 for ALL 12 Major pentatonic scales and ALL 12 minor pentatonic scales.

CHAPTER 7

TUNE IN

"I am a musician and a guitar player. Music is my language and my guitar is my voice. Music is Melody, Harmony and Rhythm. I develop my language skills and my instrument skills. They are two separate worlds working together to complete the circle of music."

Rhythm is the number one factor to sounding great as a musician.

WARM UP

MSL 6 strings   Quarter-notes and Eighth-notes   60-90 BPM *(not written)*

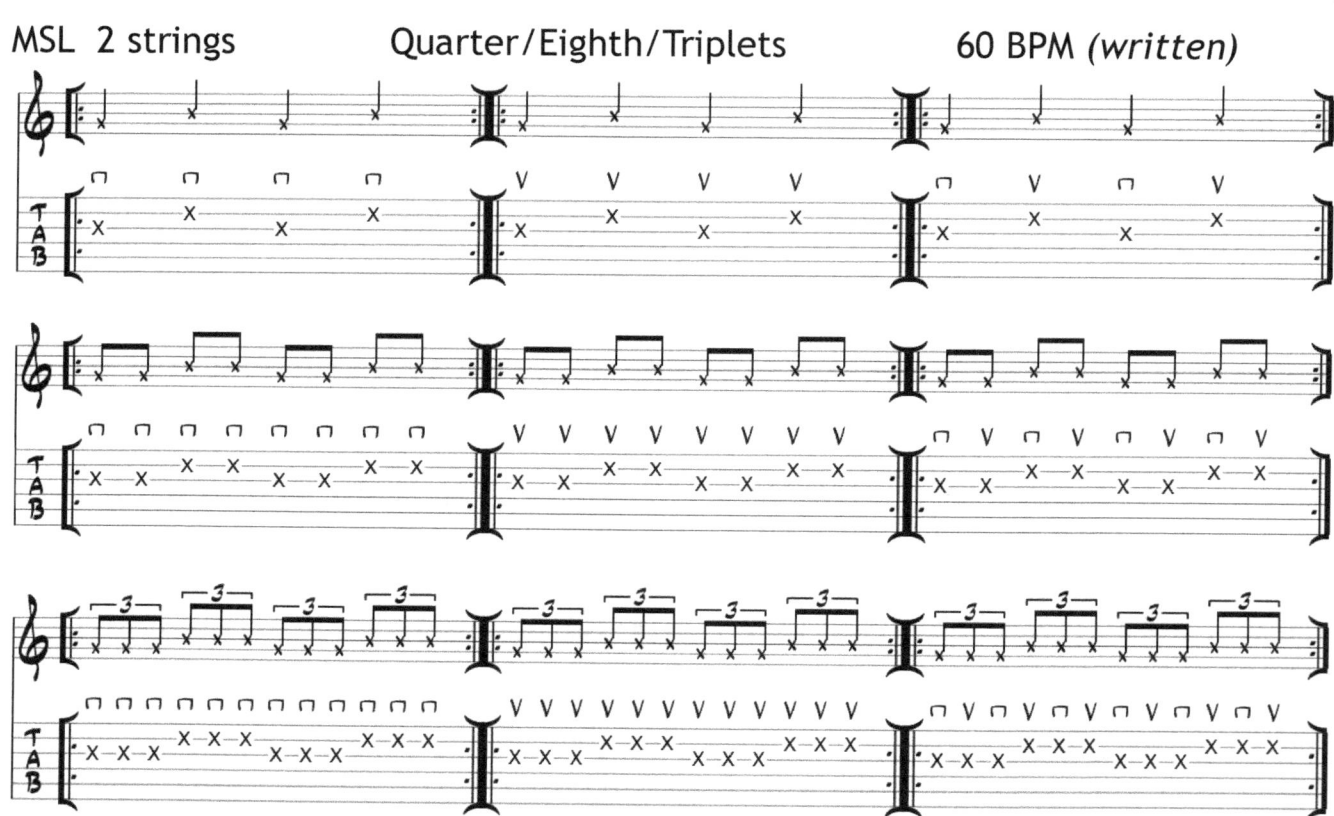

MSL 2 strings   Quarter/Eighth/Triplets   60 BPM *(written)*

SHELL

1 2 3 4   Quarter-notes   60 BPM

REVIEW

When we first see a chord progression we try to figure out the "main" chord. You can look for what chord it starts with, ends with, or what chord has the most instances. But the deciding factor is which chord in the progression SOUNDS like it resolves to. Which chord is the one you would end on in a performance? Usually you will have to play through the chords a few times and your ear should tell you which one.

Here is a new BACKING TRACK to work on.

$\frac{4}{4}$| **Am** |**G** |**F** |**G** ||

1) Find the "main" chord. In this case it is the Am chord. (A minor chord equals an A minor pentatonic scale.)

2) Find the A note on the E string. (A is on the 5th fret)

3) Use the Rock and Roll Rule and put your **first finger** on the **A** to make pattern #1 a minor scale from that A note.

4) Lay your hand down in the Traditional "Stance" (chapter #1) to help you get in a good position to play. (Your pinky will be on the 8th fret.)

5) Start playing Pattern #1 from the first finger (the minor root A). It will sound (and be) an A minor pentatonic scale and you will have 2 octaves of notes to use. Remember where the minor roots are, think the "V" shape (chapter #3).

Use an A minor pentatonic scale for practice.
Use the (2) A minor pentatonic LICKS to start to solo

For the follow-along BACKING TRACK VIDEO visit
www.LeadGuitarWorkshop.com

EXERCISE

Pattern #1 A minor/C Major   Quarter-notes   60 BPM

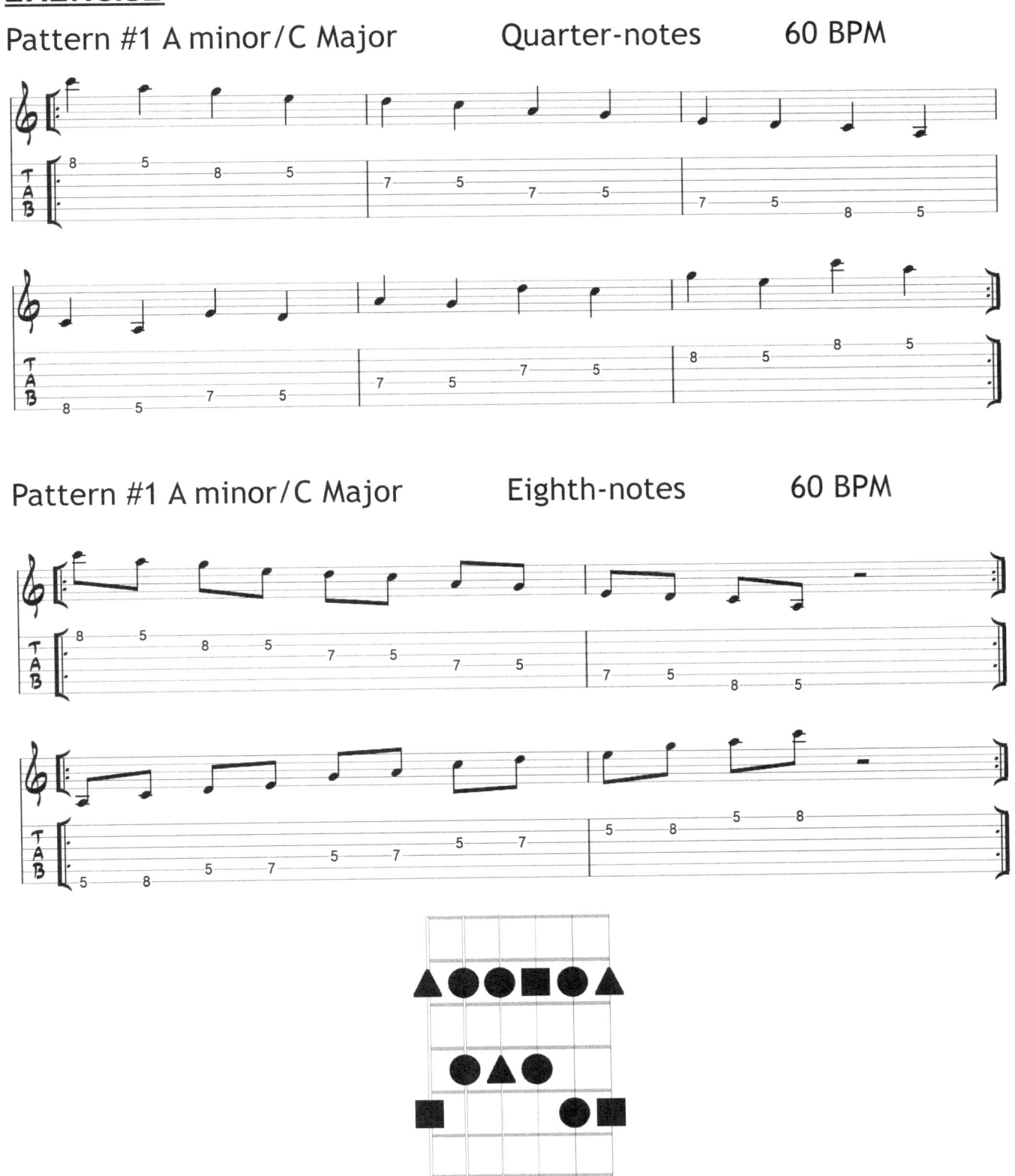

Pattern #1 A minor/C Major   Eighth-notes   60 BPM

LICKS Am/C

Here are the *same* licks we have done in Pattern #1 in A minor and C Major (Pattern #1 from the 5th-8th frets). They are transposed to the key of A minor and C Major (which are relatives). These licks "trace" the same way for except for the open strings. The Em/G key is the only one with Pattern #1 using open strings. All eleven other keys will "trace" or feel the same. Only the starting fret/note changes.

Minor Licks (A minor)

Higher Octave

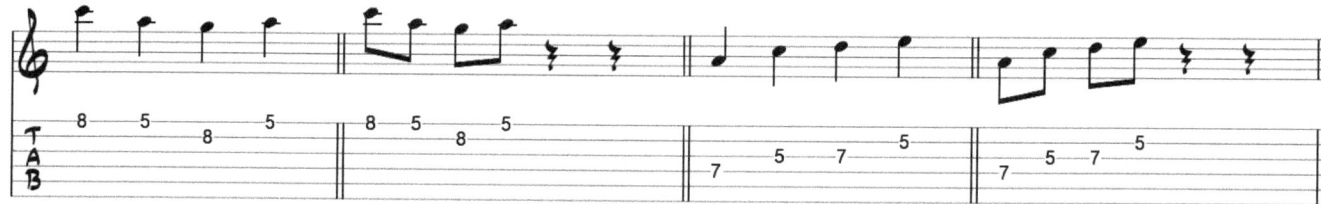

Lower Octave

Major Licks (C Major)

Higher Octave

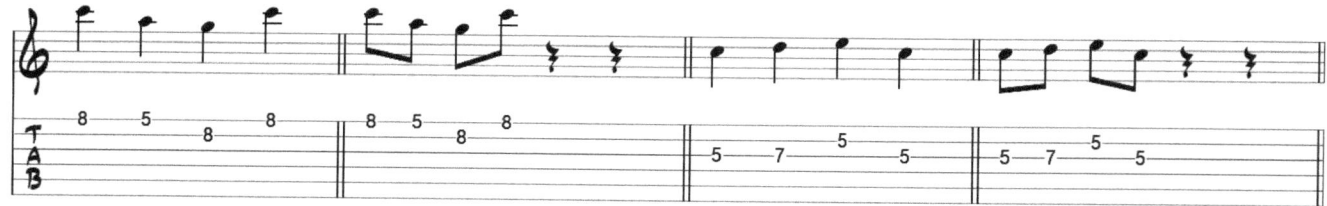

Lower Octave

BLUE NOTE

The Blue Note is a very famous note. It's so famous that a Jazz Record Label was named after it and the jazz club on West 4th Street in NYC was named after it. To me the Blue Note is like hot sauce. It isn't part of the original meal but it really spices it up. And like hot sauce, too much can negate its effect.

The Blue Note is not part of the scale or the key. It is an additional note we add to create a bluesy, sassy and salty sound. It is in all styles of music from Jazz to metal, funk to bluegrass. It is the main color note in the melody of Duke Ellington's "It Don't Mean A Thing," and it's in the main riff of Metallica's "Enter Sandman."

The Blue Note creates a lot of tension. It's normally used as a passing tone and not a landing tone. It needs to keep moving and it needs to go to another note to resolve.

OPEN Pattern #1 **Em/G** with Blue Note	Pattern #1 **Am/C** with Blue Note (5thfret)

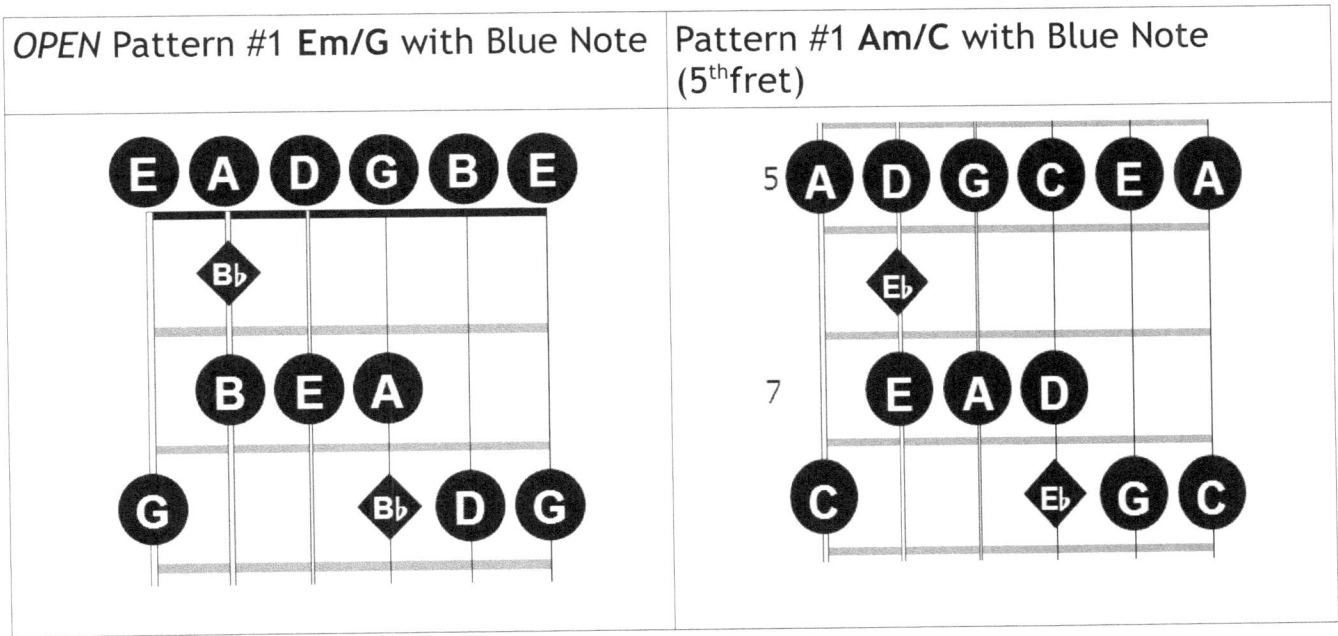

The Blue Note is always in the same physical place in Pattern #1. (That is one of the easy things for guitarists.) The names of the notes change but it will feel and act the same in different keys.

You should notice that the Blue Note happens once in each octave. Some folks mistakenly think there are two Blue Notes, when in fact, it's one note in two octaves.

PRACTICE

PATTERN #1 OPEN (G/Em)

Major Blue Note Lick   2 octaves   Quarters/Eighths (G Major)

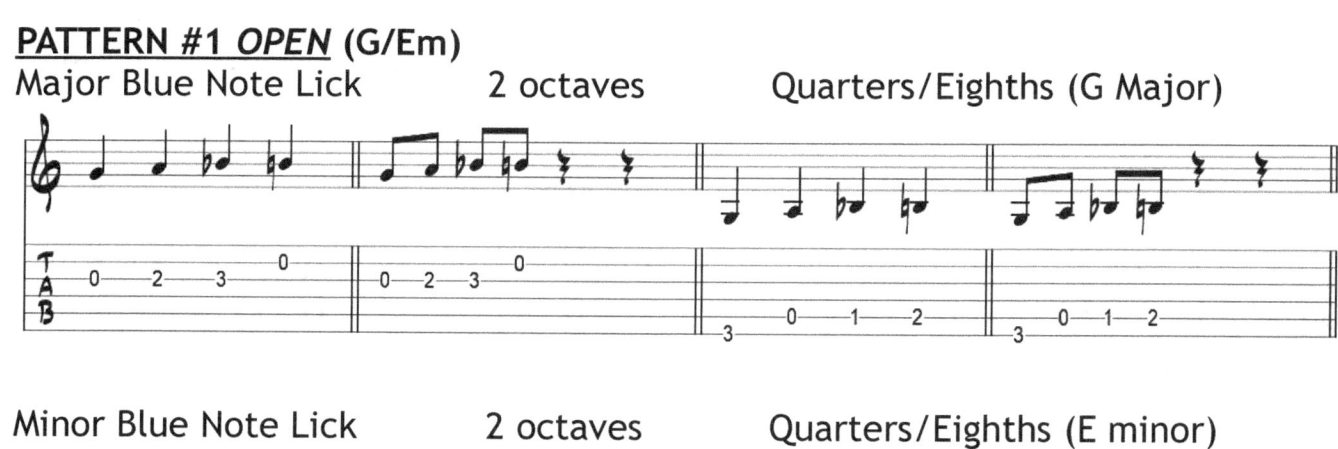

Minor Blue Note Lick   2 octaves   Quarters/Eighths (E minor)

PATTERN #1 MOVEABLE (C/Am)

Major Blue Note Lick   2 octaves   Quarters/Eighths (C Major)

Minor Blue Note Lick   2 octaves   Quarters/Eighths (A minor)

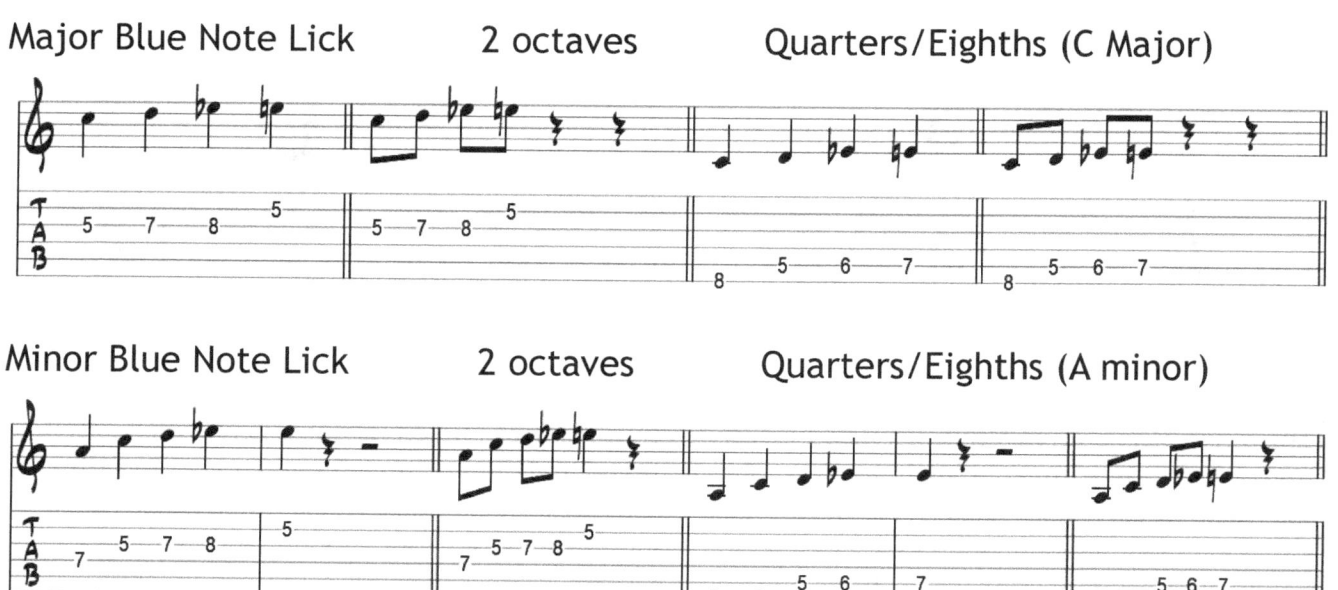

BACKING TRACKS-ALL

Backing Track- G Major G Major pentatonic scale G Major licks	**RELATIVES** G Major/E minor Pattern #1 OPEN
Backing Track- E Minor E minor pentatonic scale E minor licks	
Backing Track- A minor A minor pentatonic scale A minor licks	**RELATIVES** C Major/A minor Pattern #1 (5th-8th fret)
Backing Track- C Major C Major pentatonic C Major licks	

SUMMARY

We are musicians.
We are guitar players.
We learn the language of music. Melody, Harmony, and Rhythm.
We learn the craft of playing the guitar as an instrument.

We warm up with Muted String Ladders (MSL) and SHELLS.

RHYTHM is most important.

We EXERCISE our scales and licks.

We learn musical ideas (LICKS) to start to build "musical conversation."

We learned what Legato is as a MUSICIAN and how to use it as a GUITAR PLAYER with HAMMER-ONS, PULL-OFFS, and SLIDES.

As a guitar player we added the King Box to extend the range of the scale.

We use BACKING TRACKS and SELF GENERATE to give a real time context to our playing.

We use PATTERN #1 Rock and Roll Rule to navigate our scales and to easily see the relationship between the Relative Major and Relative minor.

As musicians we always remember keys/chords/scales are a "two-for-one deal." When you remember relative Major you know the relative minor. There are only 12 of these relationships in all of music.

You will use Pattern #1 for ALL 12 Major pentatonic scales and ALL 12 minor pentatonic scales, one for each fret.

Don't forget that at the 12th fret the guitar (an music world) start over again an octave higher. That means for the Keys of Em/G (12th-15th fret) up to Bm/D (19th-22nd fret) you get Pattern #1 an octave higher.

CHAPTER 8

TUNE IN

"I am a musician and a guitar player. Music is my language and my guitar is my voice. Music is Melody, Harmony and Rhythm. I develop my language skills and my instrument skills. They are two separate worlds working together to complete the circle of music."

Rhythm is the number one factor to sounding great as a musician.

WARM UP

MSL 6 strings   Quarter-notes/Eighth-notes   60-90 BPM (not written)

MSL 3 strings   Quarters/Eighths/triplets   60 BPM (written)

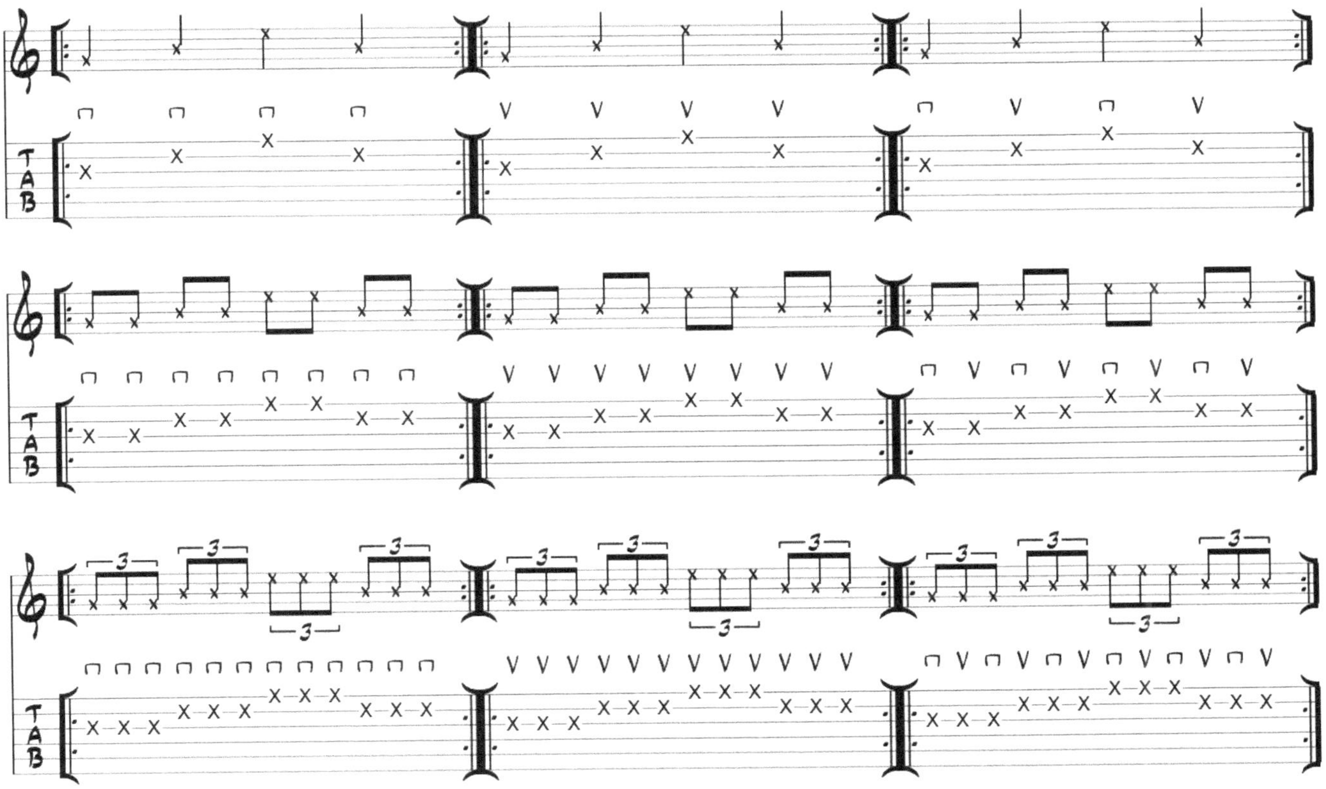

SHELLS 1 2 3 4   Quarter-notes   60 BPM (not written)
            1 2 3 4   Eighth-notes   60 BPM (written)

SHELL 1 2 3 Triplets

EXERCISE

Pattern #1 OPEN G/Em with Blue Note　　　Eighth-notes

Pattern #1 C/Am with Blue Note　　　Eighth-notes

LICKS

PATTERN #1 *OPEN* (G/Em)

Major Blue Note Lick　　　2 octaves　　　Quarters/Eighths (G Major)

Minor Blue Note Lick　　　2 octaves　　　Quarters/Eighths (E minor)

PATTERN #1 *MOVEABLE* (C/Am)

REVIEW

The Blue Note is an artificial note that's not supposed to work but does! It's a very familiar sound and it happens in Major and minor pentatonics. We added the Blue Note (a 6th note) to our pattern #1 and now we can see it in the King Box too, giving us a third octave of the Blue Note. We can see how the Blue Note is in the same physical location even in other keys. That makes it easy to remember and easy to feel how it responds to the surrounding notes.

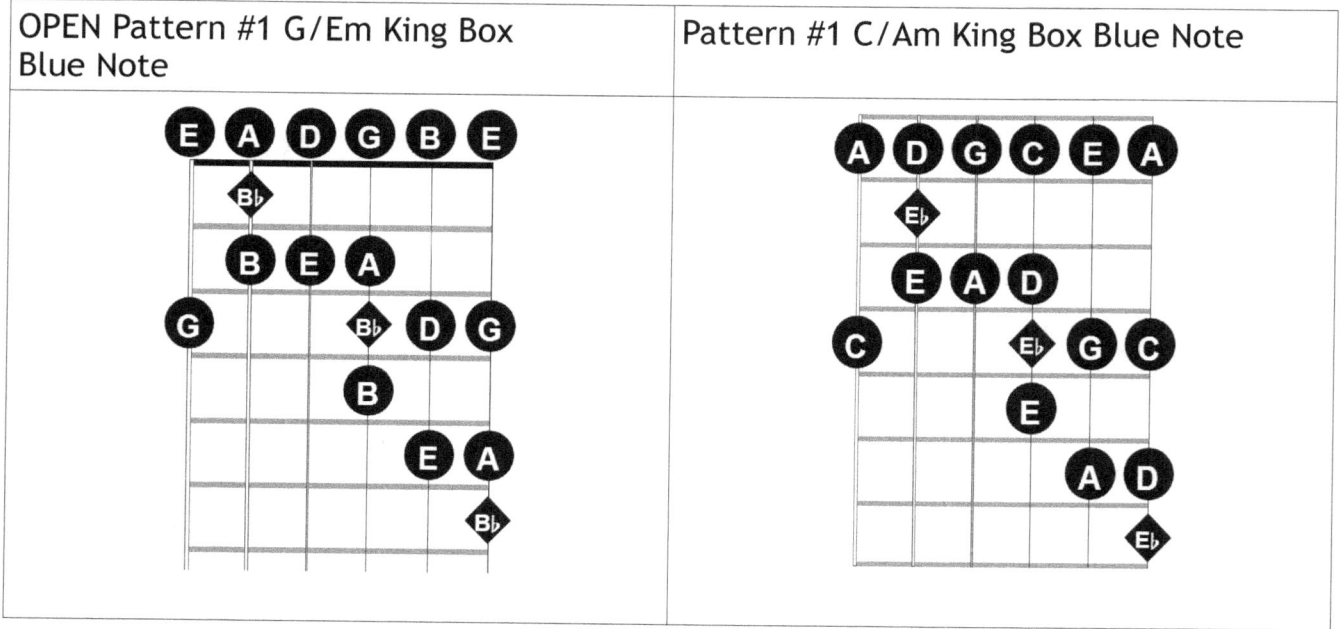

BENDING

Bending is one of the coolest things we can do on guitar and it's what makes other instrumentalists really envious. Bending gives us the ability to go between the notes and connect them in a way similar to the human voice. The real advantage we have as guitarists is that we can control how much we bend the note. We can control the interval or distance between notes created by the bend, and we can control the sustain and release of the bend.

Bending is another technique we use to perform *legato* on the guitar (in addition to Hammer-ons, Pull-offs, and slides).

Bending is by far the most difficult of the techniques, both physically and musically.

HOW TO BEND:

1. Use third finger to play a note (example 5th fret on high E string).
2. Put middle finger on the previous fret, same string, right behind third finger. This is there to help push/leverage the string.
3. Keep thumb on top of the fretboard binding. (This is the BLUES grip covered in Chapter #1.)
4. Pluck note, *turn wrist to hook note* with curled fingers to push string up. You should hear the note go up. Don't expand/contract the fingers.

SETUP	BEND
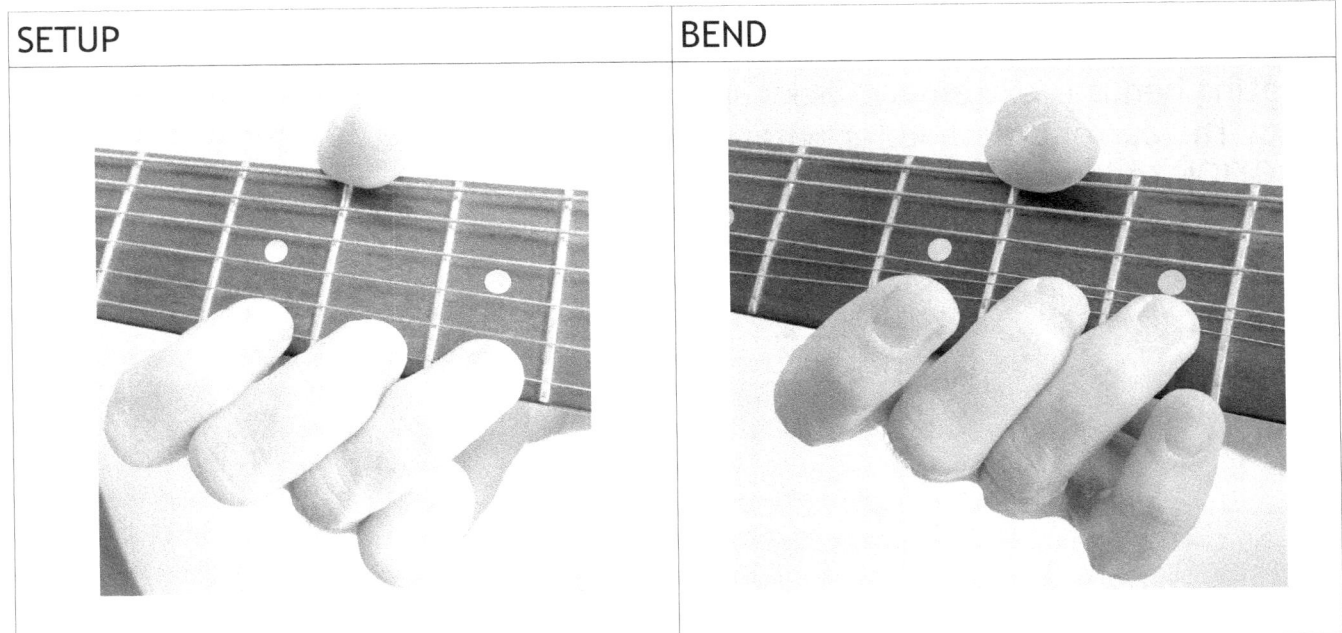	

BENDING

When I first started playing I thought bends just "sweetened" the note. But sometimes my bends were good, sometimes amazing and sometimes they sounded like drunk ducks falling out the sky. It took me a while to realize that (musically) we are changing notes when we bend. It's hard to see because we stay on the same fret when we bend. If you *listen*, then you will hear the note not only going up but becoming the note on the next fret. This is know as a **HALF-STEP BEND.**

When we bend a note up it changes to the next note. If we release the bend it goes back to the original note. Therefore there are TWO types of basic bends: BEND, and BEND and RELEASE.

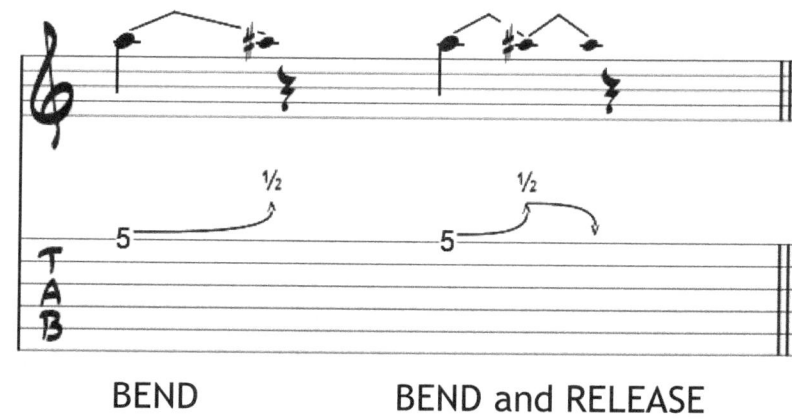

BEND   BEND and RELEASE

Notating bends is extremely tricky and people/software do it in different ways. The current method for notating bends is using and ARROW and a FRACTION to indicate the interval or distance for the bend. Above is GUITAR PRO and below is MUSESCORE show a BEND.

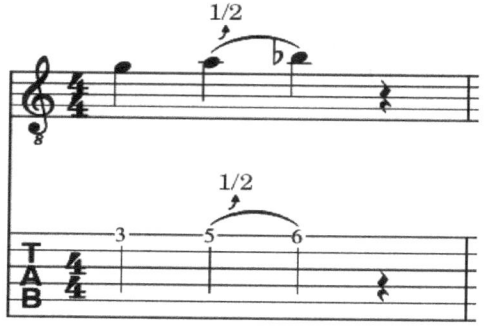

BENDING

There are different intervals that we use in bending and they are indicated with fractions.

1/4	**NOT a new note** just "lifts the sound" of the note
1/2	Half-step = **1 fret**
Full	Whole-step = **2 frets**
Step+1/2	Whole-step plus half-step = **3 frets**
2 Full	(2) whole-steps = **4 frets**

PRACTICE

The only way to play a bend correctly is to do it by ear. It's hard but it is the only way. To practice this, play the musical idea without the bend and then play it with the bend to match the pitch.

At first, instead of bending the note with the third finger, simply move up a fret (same finger) and play the note and then go back a fret. Then do it again BUT with a bend instead. They should sound (almost) the same.

Play NORMAL   play with BEND

SELF GEN

Here is our SELF-GENERATING method of playing (practicing). It's one bar of a chord and one bar of a lick/solo.

Here are the previous two bending licks: BEND, and BEND and RELEASE.
Each one is shown with G Major chords and E minor chords

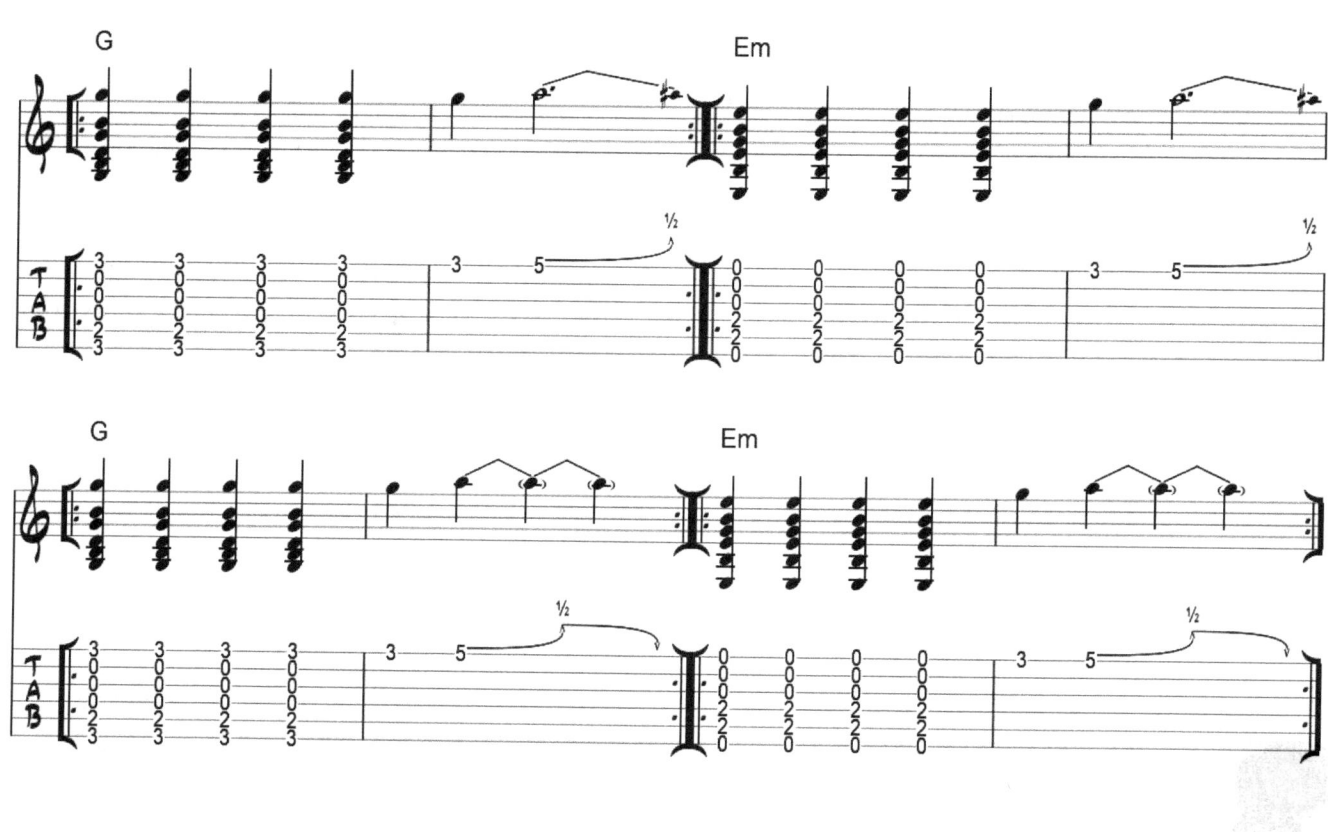

SUMMARY

We are musicians. We are guitar players.
We learn the language of music. Melody, Harmony, and Rhythm.
We learn the craft of playing the guitar as an instrument.

We warm up with Muted String Ladders (MSL) and SHELLS.

RHYTHM is most important.

We EXERCISE our scales and licks.

We learn musical ideas (LICKS) to start to build "musical conversation."

We learned what Legato is as a MUSICIAN and how to use it as a GUITAR
PLAYER with HAMMER-ONS, PULL-OFFS, SLIDES, and BENDS.

As a guitar player we added the King Box to extend the range of the scale.

We use BACKING TRACKS and SELF GENERATE to give a real time context to our
playing.

We use PATTERN #1 Rock and Roll Rule to navigate our scales and to easily see
the relationship between the Relative Major and Relative minor.

As musicians we always remember keys/chords/scales are a "two-for-one
deal." When you remember relative Major you know the relative minor. There
are only 12 of these relationships in all of music.

We have the BLUE NOTE to add some "salt and spice" to our sound. It works in
Major and minor.

You will use Pattern #1 for ALL 12 Major pentatonic scales and ALL 12 minor
pentatonic scales, one for each fret.

Don't forget that at the 12th fret the guitar (an music world) start over again
an octave higher. That means for the Keys of Em/G (12th-15th fret) up to Bm/D
(19th-22nd fret) you get Pattern #1 an octave higher.

CHAPTER 9

TUNE IN

"I am a musician and a guitar player. Music is my language and my guitar is my voice. Music is Melody, Harmony and Rhythm. I develop my language skills and my instrument skills. They are two separate worlds working together to complete the circle of music."

Rhythm is the number one factor to sounding great as a musician.

WARM UP

MSL 6 strings   Quarters/Eighths   *(not written)* 60 BPM
MSL 2 String   all 4 gears/Rhythms   *(written)* 60 BPM

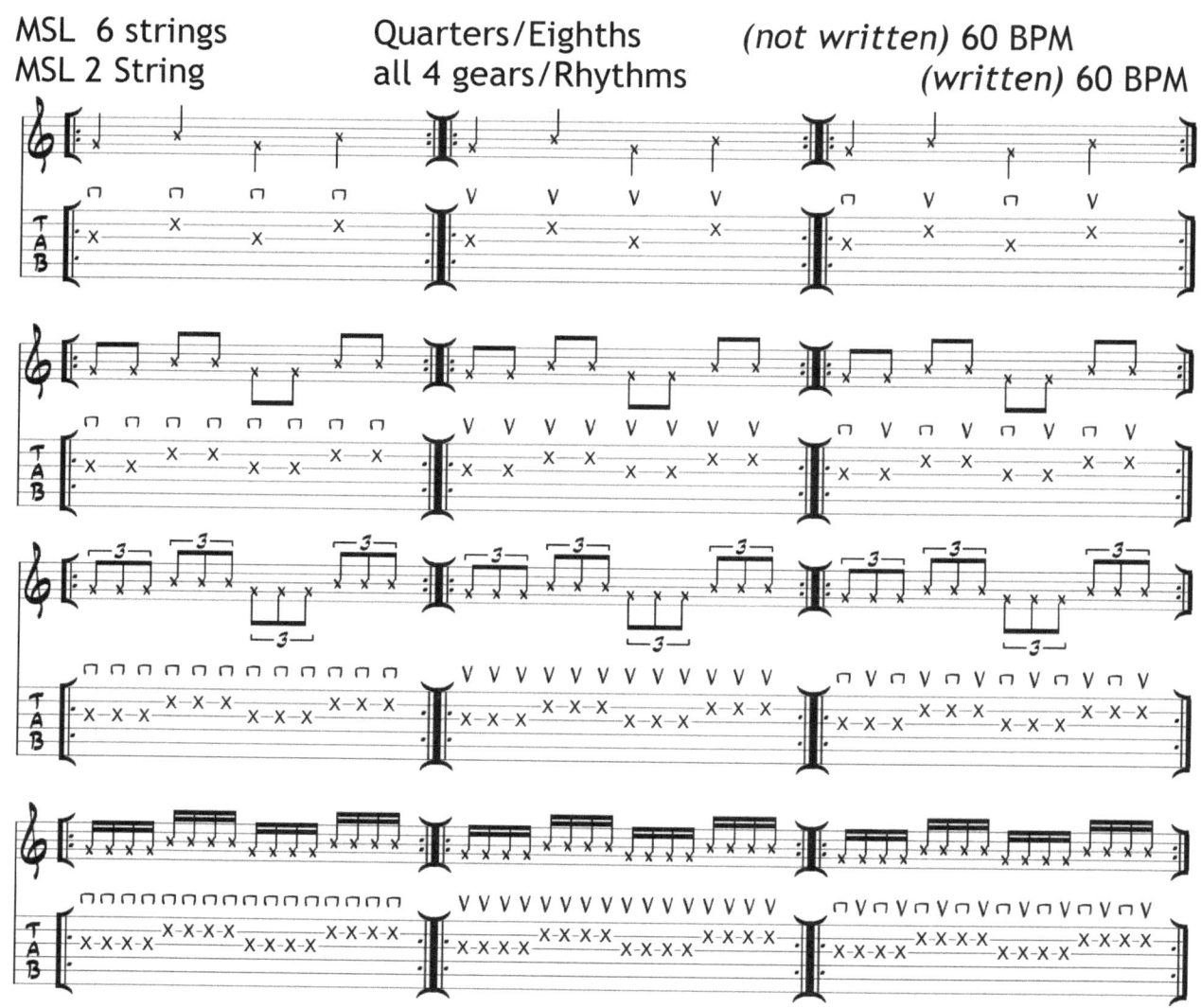

SHELLS

SHELL 2 4	Quarter-notes and Eighth-notes	60BPM *(not written)*
SHELL 2 3 4	Quarter-notes	60BPM *(not written)*
SHELL 1 3 w HO PO	Quarter-notes	60 BPM *(written)*

Hammer-ons for the 13 part and pull-offs for the 31 part

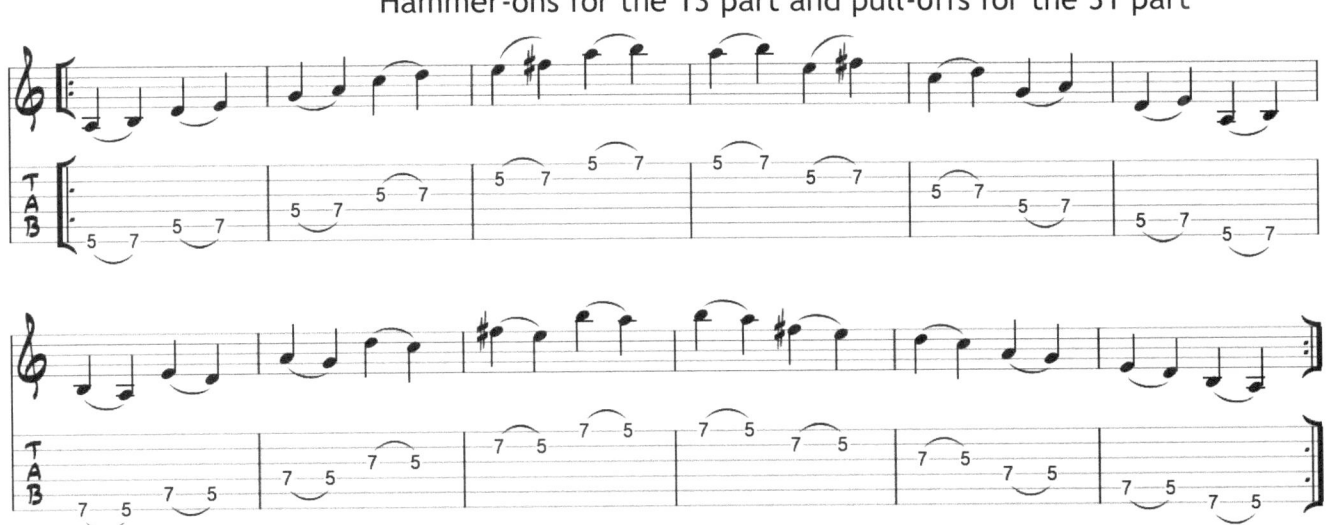

EXERCISE

Pattern #1 Eighth-notes	60 BPM, *Play in different Keys/frets (not written)*
Pattern #1 Quarter-notes	Key of C/Am, HO PO, Shell style 60 BPM *(written)*

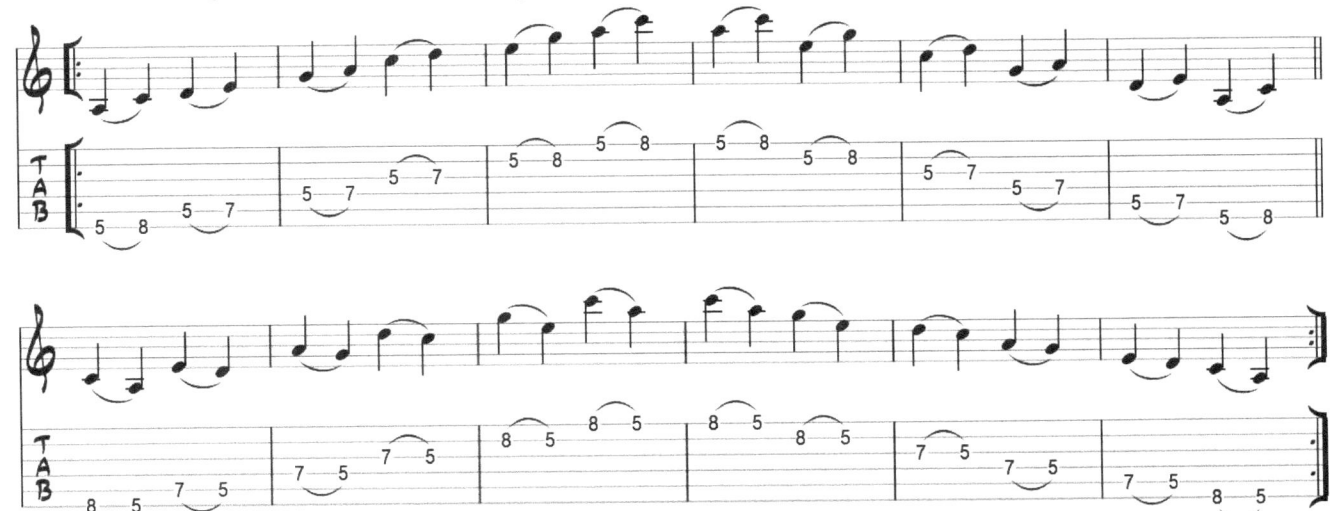

REVIEW

Self Generate: Bending licks E minor and G Major

Self Generate: Bending licks A minor and C Major

PATTERN #2

To further move our notes up the neck we need to learn more shapes to play the *same* notes. Even though it looks and feels very different than pattern #1, Pattern #2 is still the **SAME SCALE** (G Major pentatonic and E minor pentatonic)

You should start with your middle finger. This pattern requires all four fingers (one finger per fret). This is the full home to the "King Box."

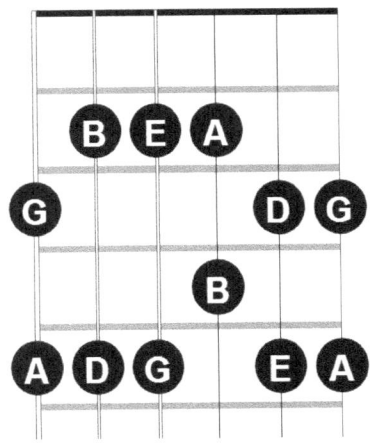

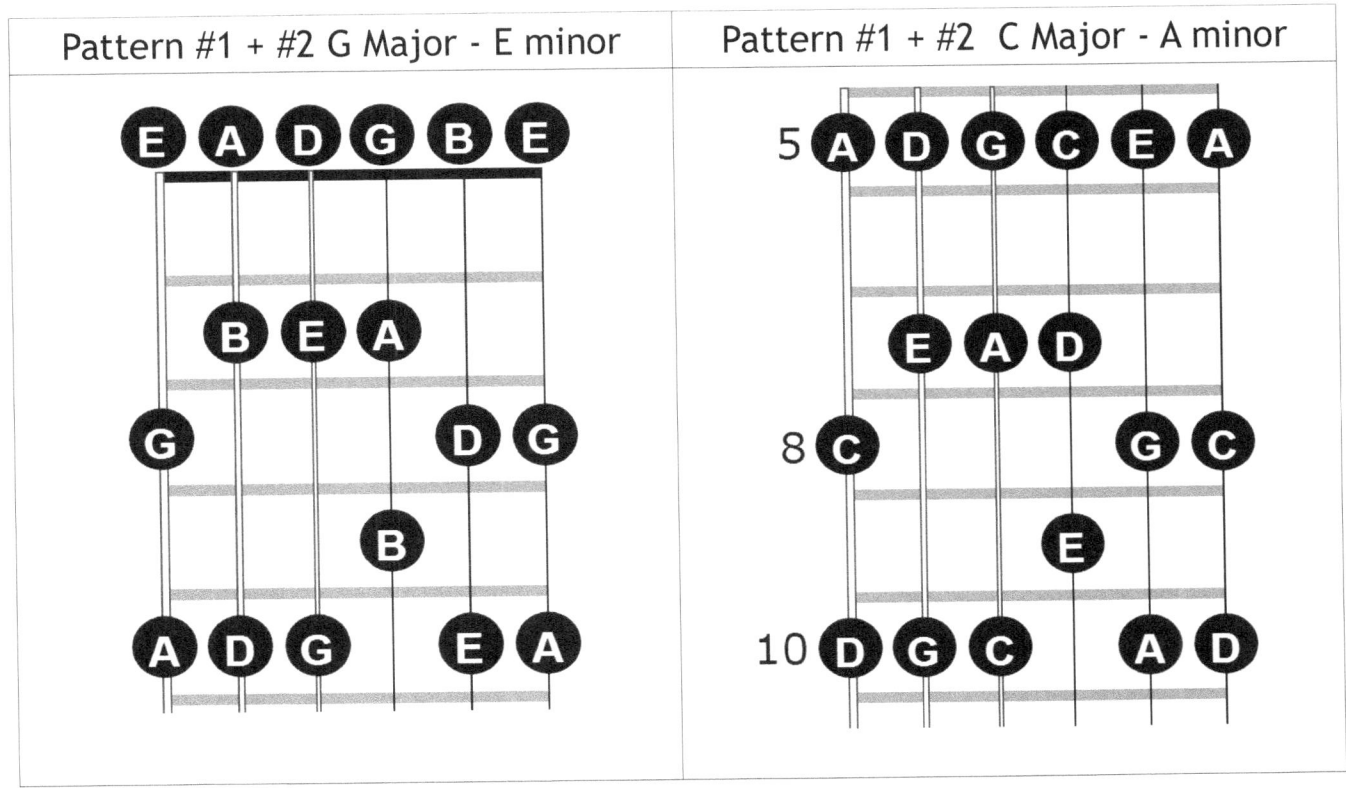

Pattern #1 + #2 G Major - E minor

Pattern #1 + #2 C Major - A minor

PRACTICE

"Around the block" is a term I use to describe ascending pattern #1, and once you hit the highest note, shift up, and start descending pattern #2 from its highest note.

Around the Bock G Major/E minor

Around the Block C Major/ A minor

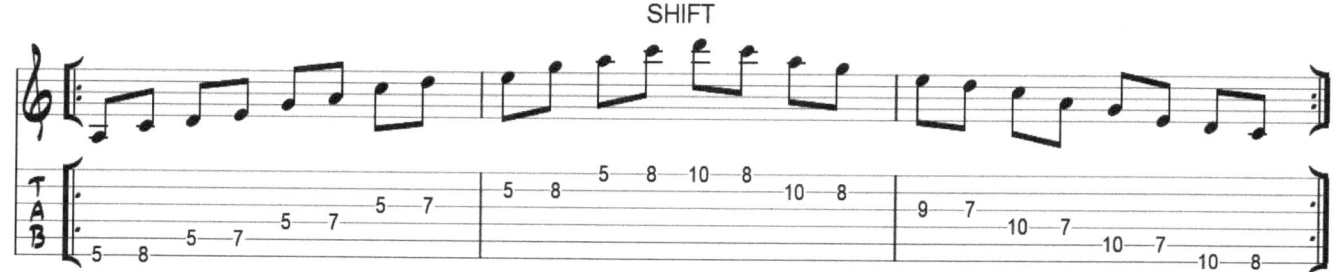

SELF GEN with LICKS Pattern #2

SUMMARY

We are musicians. We are guitar players.
We learn the language of music. Melody, Harmony, and Rhythm.
We learn the craft of playing the guitar as an instrument.

We warm up with Muted String Ladders (MSL) and SHELLS.

RHYTHM is most important.

We EXERCISE our scales and licks.

We learn musical ideas (LICKS) to start to build "musical conversation."

We learned about Relative Major and Relative minor as a two-for-one in music. One scale is two. We use the ROCK AND ROLL RULE for pattern #1 to help us guitarists see this musical relationship.

We learned what LEGATO is as a MUSICIAN and how to use it as a GUITAR PLAYER with HAMMER-ONS, PULL-OFF'S, SLIDES, and BENDS.

We use BACKING TRACKS and SELF GENERATE to give a real time context to our playing.

We use PATTERN #1 Rock and Roll Rule to navigate our scales and to easily see the relationship between the Relative Major and Relative minor.

We added PATTERN #2 (home of the King Box) to extend the scales up the neck to allow for slides and other articulations.

We have the BLUE NOTE to add some "salt and spice" to our sound. It works in Major and minor.

You will use Pattern #1 to navigate ALL 12 Major pentatonic scales and ALL 12 minor pentatonic scales, one for each fret.

Don't forget that at the 12th fret the guitar (and music world) start over again an octave higher. That means for the Keys of Em/G (12th - 15th fret) up to Bm/D (19th - 22nd fret) you get Pattern #1 an octave higher.

CHAPTER 10

TUNE IN

You are growing in two ways. You grow as a musician, understanding the language, and you grow as a guitar player, a crafts person on an instrument. Those skills will grow simultaneously but separately. Each helps the other avoid confusion about music or instrument related questions. If you ask a guitar player how many notes are in an Am chord they might (incorrectly) answer "five." The music answer is three, because there are only three notes in a triad. But a guitar player has five strings in the open A minor chord, and two of the notes are duplicated in the voicing. When confronted with an unknown you must ask yourself:

Is this a music question or a guitar question?

"How many notes are in an A minor chord?" "three"
"How many strings do I strum for an A minor chord?" "five"

Sometimes it seems so obvious, but often it won't. You have to ask yourself about what are you really trying to find an answer for. Once you know the music language and all of its questions and answers it's the same with any instrument. You just have to physically adapt the information to the instrument.

"The student as a boxer and not a fencer. The fencer's weapon is picked up and put down again. The boxer's is part of him. All he has to do is clench his fist."

This quote by *Marcus Aurelius* really struck me. I immediately thought,

"The student as a musician and not a guitarist. A guitarist picks up and puts down his instrument. The musician's is part of him. All he has to do is tap, clap and sing."

WARM UP REVIEW

MUTED STRING LADDERS (MSL) are a fantastic warm up that exercise the picking hand and your rhythmic abilities.

- Choose how many strings (1-6). Mute strings with fretboard hand.
- Start with quarter-notes. Then change rhythm or "gears" to eighth-notes, then triplets, then sixteenth-notes.
- Start with ALL DOWN picks.
- Change to ALL UP picks.
- Change to ALTERNATE picking.
- Change to NEXT GEAR/RHYTHM

MSL 6 strings 60 BPM All four RHYTHMS (GEARS)

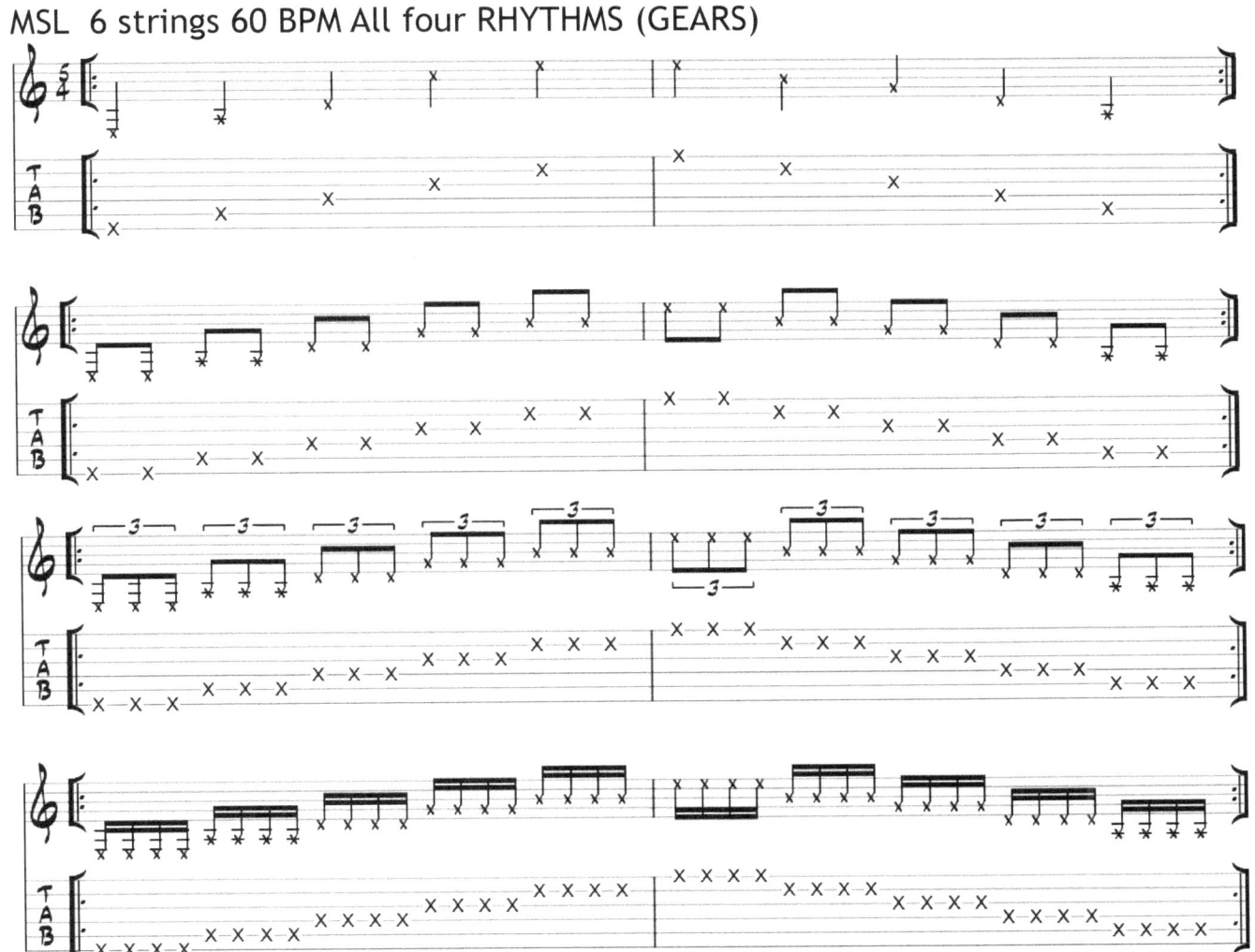

SHELL Review

Shells are like "wax on, wax off's." They are actions that practice real world moves. These exercises help you in real musical situations. They also help you overcome guitar hindrances. These are *not* scale exercises *but* dexterity exercises. Any time you are having a fingering issue you can make a shell out of it to help you. Your musicianship should not be dictated by finger habits.

- Choose any combination of fingers (for example 1 2 3 4)
- Pick a RHYTHM and a starting fret.
- You will use that fingering (1 2 3 4) to ascend and (1 2 3 4) to descend.
- Then REVERSE the fingering (4 3 2 1) and ascend and descend with same (4 3 2 1).

SHELL 1 2 3 4 Eighth-notes

EXERCISE REVIEW

Exercising scales and licks are an effective bridge between physical warm-ups and musical duties. It's really helpful to Self-Generate the chord and then play the scale/lick. It's great for your ear, your rhythm, your feel, and your overall ability to carry the tune.

G Major

E minor

REVIEW MUSIC and GUITAR

MUSICIAN	GUITAR PLAYER
Pentatonic Scale Five note scale that has two inherent sounds, Major and minor. In the key of G Major the notes are G A B D E.	Pattern #1 G/Em *open* Pattern #2 G/Em
Relative Major and minor When the starting note is G the scale sounds like a Major scale (G A B D E). When the scale starts on the E, it sounds like a minor pentatonic. (E G A B D)	 Pattern #1 Pattern #1 Major root note minor root note
Legato is the smooth transition of one note to another without any silence between the notes. It is an even, flowing sound.	 HO PO Slide Bend

MUSICIAN	GUITAR PLAYER

MUSICIAN

There are **12 notes** in all of music. 7 natural notes and 5 accidental notes. Each one of them is a key/chord/scale. There are 12 Major pentatonic scales (one for each note) and 12 minor pentatonic scales (one for each note). For a musician, it's a two-for-one deal. Every Major has a relative minor and vice-versa. There are **12 Relative Major-minor relationships** in all of music.

TRIANGLE = *minor* ROOT
SQUARE = *Major* ROOT

GUITAR PLAYER

Rock and Roll Rule

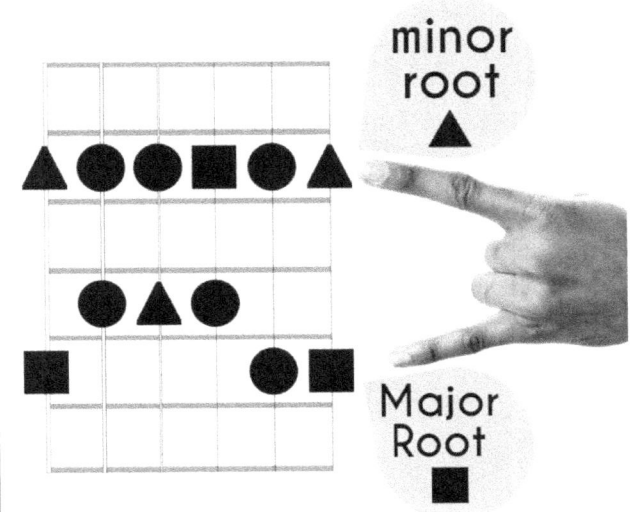

minor root ▲

Major Root ■

Once you know the chord progression you are going to solo over, you must decide on the **"MAIN" CHORD** (the chord the others revolve around and want to resolve to). **Then you match the scale to the chord, Major=Major and minor=minor.**

Find the root of the chord (6th string).

Decide on **INDEX** for minor or **PINKY** for Major.

Match the finger to the fret and lay down pattern #1.

Pattern # 1 MOVEABLE

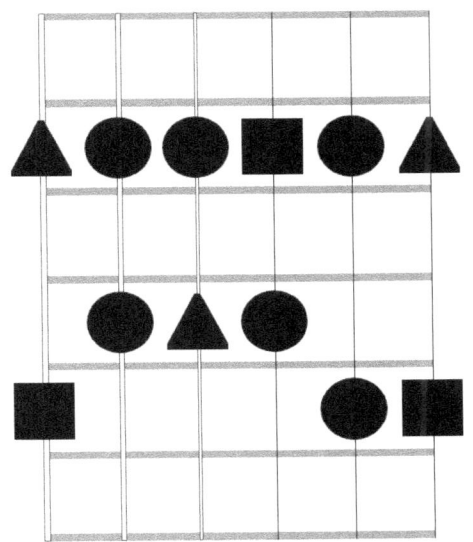

LICKS REVIEW

The Core licks #1 an #2   G Major and E minor   two-octaves

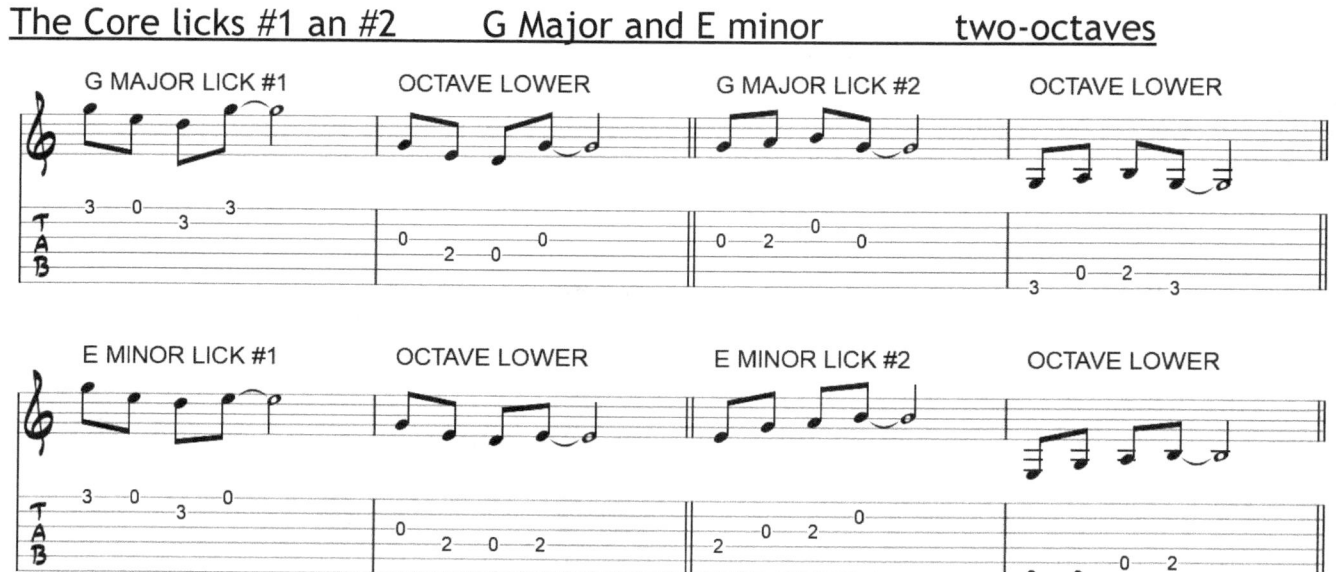

Variations on Lick #1 with articulations

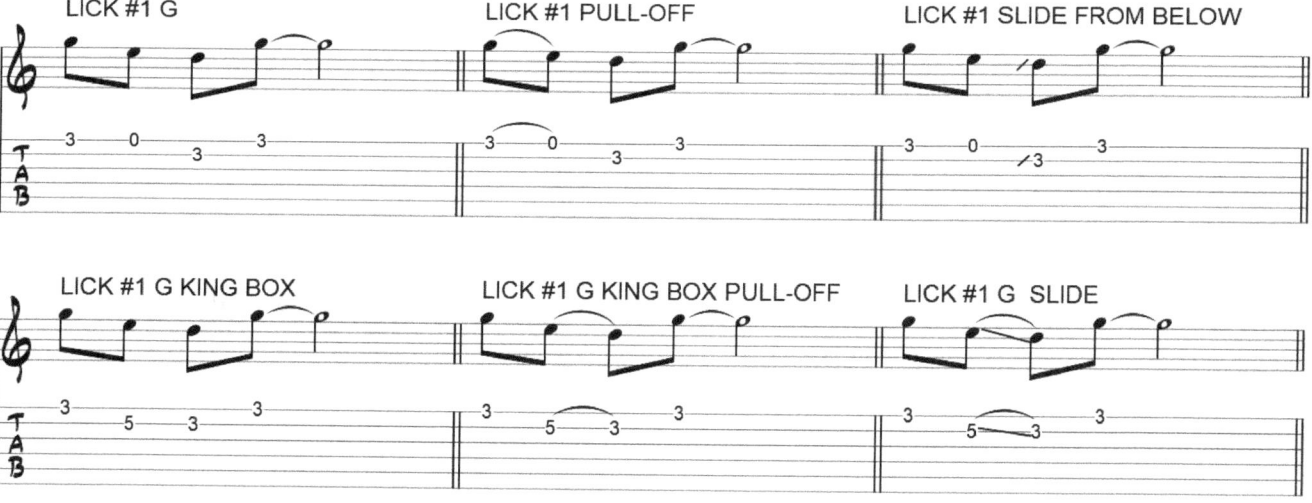

LICKS

THE 1-2 SLIDE Is the most common "pathway" for connecting Pattern #1 and the King Box/Pattern #2. This lick has endless variations and is the backbone to most guitar solos.

G Major 1-2 Slide as Quarter-notes and Eighth-notes

E minor 1-2 Slide as Quarter-notes and Eighth-notes

LICK VARIATIONS

Once you have a few licks up and going the next step is to vary them. Often in music the idea we are looking for is already in our heads/hands. We have to ask more of what we are already doing instead of looking elsewhere.
One of the most effective ways to do this is with **CALL AND RESPONSE.** This is a question and an answer. You play a lick and then a variation of it. One way to start is to change the last note of the lick. You can flip flop last two notes, or add notes. You can change the rhythm or duplicate notes. There are no rules as to how you vary a lick. That is some of the fun part.
Here are TWO examples of a Call and Response.

This works even better when you have TWO variations and make the Call and Response twice as long. You can think of the phrases as **A B A C.**

HOW TO PRACTICE

One of the best ways to practice is not to practice but to play. Practice makes it feel like it's a preparation for some future event, when in reality you are playing music now. So treat it like that.

SELF-GENERATING is my term for playing one bar of chords and one bar of a scale/lick/riff. The idea is very flexible and can be made to fit almost anything you are trying to improve. It does it in a way that is real music. It is the same process you will use to play music by yourself unaccompanied. Turn on the music, the feel, and the groove yourself. Make someone start tapping their foot.

You can play anything for the chords that you are comfortable with or trying to learn. This can help your chord playing too by incorporating bar chords, chord inversions, arpeggios.

With any chord, you can think of the full chord as having different parts like a drum kit. The low couple of strings are the KICK drum and the HIGH strings act like the snare. You can selectively strum the chords as a drum beat, BOOM, CHIK, BOOM BOOM CHIK. (This is happening in the example below.)

SELF-GEN E minor using TWO Call and Responses.

HOW TO PRACTICE

Tune in - 5%
Take a few minutes to clear your head. Turn off your devices and do what you need before you dig in and play. Remind yourself that you are a musician and a guitar player. Everything you play should be rhythmically based, always.

Warm up - 10%
Muted String Ladders, Shells, and Changing Gears are some of the best warm ups. They simply get your fingers, hands, and internal clock all synchronized. Muted String ladders focus on rhythm and pick control. Changing Gears really harnesses the ability to feel and play rhythms. The Shells are best of both worlds and are like "wax on, wax off." Practice real world moves and patterns.

Exercise - 15%
This is where you run scales and patterns. This is a great opportunity to play through the five patterns. Always play them in time and play them ascending and descending or as "Round the Block" zigzag the patterns.

Review - 15%
Just as important as learning something new, make sure your'e understanding something you have recently learned. It's essential to build your growth by reviewing past topics and understanding them deeper.

New Topic - 15%
Learn something new. However easy or small, it is growth. Every little bit moves you towards your goal of sounding great as a musician. Maybe it's learning the names of the notes in a scale, or a lick, a chord, anything that helps you sound better. You can learn as a musician, as a guitar player, and as a rhythmist.

"Practice" - 40%
The best way to practice is not to practice, but to play! It's true. Every one of our heroes played music more than anything else. Practicing refers to some future date that you are preparing for. Playing is now. Play in time, carry the song, the beat, the groove, all of it. Self-Generating is the best way to play and get your practicing in. If you are practicing a turnaround in a blues, then you play the 12 bar blues and at the end you play the turnaround. If you miss it, keep playing and get it the next time around. This is what you would do onstage. Keep playing and you will get better, as you would if you "practiced."

THOUGHTS

The learning path in music is circular. You will learn something and come back around to it and get to know it better. Every time you do this you will gain more confidence and experience. There is only so much actual information you will need to learn. It is all about how to use and manipulate that material that makes the magic of music start. Learning music is not a linear path but a circular one.

Music is Melody (notes), Harmony (chords), and Rhythm.
Rhythm is the number one factor to sounding great.

Where attention goes, energy flows. So much of being a better musician is all about your mind set and what you focus your time and energy on.

"The process of learning consists not in what is brought to the learner, but what is drawn out of him." (Plato)

"The Student as a boxer, not a fencer. The Fencer's weapon is picked up and put down again. The Boxer's is part of him, all he has to do is clench his fist." (Marcus Aurelius-Meditations)

"The Student as a musician, not a guitarist. The guitarist's instrument is picked up and put down. The musician's is part of him. All he has to do is tap, clap, and sing." (Suke Cerulo)

You can play music without melody (just chords) and you can play music without chords (just melody, like your voice), but you can *never* play music without rhythm, it's impossible. As soon as you tap your foot or pluck a note, rhythm happens.

The language of music hasn't really changed in hundreds of years. It is much older than the guitar. Once you know the language, that's it. Now you can learn as many instruments as you want. You just have to adapt to the physical part of the instrument.

The instrument is silent without you. You are music!

BACKING TRACKS-ALL

Another extremely enjoyable way to play is to jam along with backing tracks. I call backing tracks HARMONIC METRONOMES. They keep a beat and also offer a harmonic backdrop (chords in the background) to give perspective to your melody notes.

The backing tracks at Lead Guitar Workshop (www.LeadGuitarWorkshop.com) are specifically created to play with, learn with and enjoy. The tracks are mostly performed live, so they don't have a "cut and paste" sound to them. They feel like a real band. They also highlight each chord played for a more advanced practice so you van "play the changes" or use arpeggios.

Backing Track- G Major G Major pentatonic scale G Major licks	<u>RELATIVES</u> G Major/E minor
Backing Track- E Minor E minor pentatonic scale E minor licks	Pattern #1 OPEN
Backing Track- C Major C Major pentatonic C Major licks	<u>RELATIVES</u> C Major/A minor
Backing Track- A minor A minor pentatonic scale A minor licks	Pattern #1 (5th-8th fret)

SUMMARY

You are a Musician and a guitar player.
We know music is Melody, Harmony and Rhythm.
We have our musical knowledge and instrumental tools.

We warm up with **Muted String Ladders (MSL)** and **SHELLS**.

RHYTHM is most important.

We Exercise our scales and licks.

We learn musical ideas (**LICKS**) to start to build "musical conversation."

We learned about Relative Major and Relative minor as a two-for-one in music. One scale is two. We use the **ROCK AND ROLL RULE** for pattern #1 to help us guitarists see this musical relationship.

We learned what **LEGATO** is as a MUSICIAN and how to use it as a GUITAR PLAYER with **HAMMER'ONS**, **PULLOFF'S**, **SLIDES**, and **BENDS**.

We use **BACKING TRACKS** and **SELF GEN** to give a real time context to our playing.

We use **PATTERN #1 Rock and Roll Rule** to navigate our scales and to easily see the relationship between the Relative Major and Relative minor.

We added **PATTERN #2** (home of the **King Box**) to extend the scales up the neck to allow for slides and other articulations.

We have the **BLUE NOTE** to add some "salt and spice" to our sound. It works in Major and minor.

You will use **Pattern #1 to navigate ALL 12 Major pentatonic scales** and **ALL 12 minor pentatonic scales**, one for each fret.

Don't forget that at the 12th fret the guitar (and music world) start over again an octave higher. That means for the Keys of Em/G (12th - 15th fret) up to Bm/D (19th - 22nd fret) you get Pattern #1 an octave higher.

Music is always happening and should be treated as such. Whenever you pick up your guitar, listen inside yourself, hear a beat, start tapping your foot and then begin to play. Even if its one chord, play it like a song. Listen to it, and make every part of it sound good. Provide a beat so strong that when someone hears you they start tapping their foot. They may even ask you what song you are playing. What you are creating is so strong it reminds the listener of somewhere else they have felt some other music. You are connecting to them and yourself.

"I am a musician and a guitar player. Music is my language and my guitar is my voice. Music is Melody, Harmony and Rhythm. I develop my language skills and my instrument skills. They are two separate worlds working together to complete the circle of music."

Rhythm is the number one factor to sounding great as a musician.

GLOSSARY

<u>Audiation</u> Inner Hearing but also the musical knowledge behind it, to hear the knowledge.

<u>Arpeggio</u> The notes of a chord played in succession rather than simultaneously.

<u>BPM</u> Beats-per-minute. How music tempo/beat/quarter-note is measured.

<u>Chord</u> Usually three or more notes played simultaneously.

<u>Chord Inversion</u> The notes of a chord rotating in order (example R35, 35R, 5R3).

<u>Chord Scale</u> The scale matched to a particular chord, using its chord tones and appropriate notes in between to best fit for playing the changes.

<u>Chord Tone</u> A single note, as part of a chord.

<u>Degree, Scale</u> The number in the scale at which a note lives. There are seven notes in the diatonic scale. They are numbered 1-7 for their degrees.

<u>Diatonic</u> meaning "of the key". Notes and chords only in that key.

<u>Diatonic Harmony</u> The seven chords that naturally occur in all keys and its resulting formula.   (I ii iii IV V vi viidim)

<u>Fingerpicking/Fingerstyle</u> Fingerpicking is using fingers only to pluck the strings on guitar. Fingerstyle might include thumb and/or fingerpicks.

<u>Gear</u> (LGW) Slang for describing the different rhythms. First gear is quarter-notes, second gear is eighth-notes; third gear is triplets; fourth gear is sixteenth-notes, and so on.

<u>Half-step</u> The smallest interval in music. It is one fret on a guitar, and a single piano key to the next (for example white to black)

Harmonic Rhythm The rhythmic pacing of chord changes; how often the chords change (for example every two beats versus every four beats).

Harmony   Chords or notes being played simultaneously to produce a sonorous sound. Chord progressions and the underlying chord motion.

HO PO Short for Hammer-ons and Pull-offs

Hybrid Picking When you combine the use of a pick and the remaining three fingers to get a combination of flat pick and fingerstyle.

Inner Hearing Hearing music in your inner ear by memory even if you don't know it musically. (Happy Birthday, Hot Cross buns, and others)

Key One of 12 families built around the 7 note Major scale. Contains 7 chords, one for each of its own notes built by the Rule of Thirds.

Legato When a musician connects the notes of a phrase in a smooth and consistent sound without any silence in between the notes.

Lick A slang term used to describe a group of notes, usually used in a lead solo. These can be recognized by style, genre, person, and more.

LGW Lead Guitar Workshop

Melody One note-at-a-time succession of notes in a pleasing fashion. The signature of a song and the part that is copyright protected.

Mode A function of a scale/key. When a Key or scale is based on any one of its chords/notes. This changes the half-steps in relation to where they live in the scale, producing varying sounds of Major and minor chord progressions and scales.

Monophonic Producing one note-at-a-time only.

Muted String Ladder (MSL)(LGW) A picking hand exercise to improve rhythm and confidence in Down, Up, and Alternate picking across the strings

Musical Truth (LGW) A term to describe some of the fundamental rules in music that every musician follows regardless of instrument.

<u>Neck Anatomy</u> (LGW) Using octaves in a short to long connection to help navigate the fretboard and move around like other instruments do and not be tied to changing patterns. There are 2 pairs of "short to long" octaves (E and A string).

<u>Pentatonic</u> Meaning "five notes of the home." These are ancient five note scales believed to have originated in Asia. There are two main types, Major and minor, and they are in all types of music all around the planet.

<u>Playing the changes</u> A slang term a musician uses when they change their note choices/scales/arpeggios to match each individual chord instead of a "Global" sound of playing one scale for all the chords.

<u>Polyphonic</u> The ability to play multiple notes simultaneously. Pianos and guitars are polyphonic, the human voice is not.

<u>Riff</u> A slang term for rhythm guitar part made up of notes instead of chords. Think "Heartbreaker" by Led Zeppelin, "Crazy Train" by Ozzy.

<u>Rhythm</u> The pulse in music. The basis for everything music. The measured beat and its subdivisions.

<u>Root</u> The "main" note in a Key/chord/scale/arpeggio. The one everything else revolves around. The sound that comes home resolves to the Root.

<u>Root Position</u> When a scale pattern, arpeggio, or chord shape has its ROOT as the lowest note.

<u>Rule of Thirds</u> Stacking every other note in a scale to create a chord. Three notes for a triad and four notes for a seventh chord.

<u>Self-Gen</u> (LGW) Using your inner ear and inner clock to start and play music yourself, in time, especially with consideration of switching between chords and soloing.

<u>Shell</u> (LGW) A hand dexterity exercise to help overcome any guitar playing issue. It involves a fingering, a performance method, and rhythm.

Staccato Each note is sharply detached or separated from the others.

Tied In music notation when an arch connects two or more rhythms to create a sustained sound. Especially useful to achieve lengths of time not possible with traditional rhythms (for example a note that last 1 ½ quarter notes.)

Tonic The "main" note/chord. Often the key but not always. It is the note/chord that everything else resolves to.

Tresillo A Latin based rhythmic figure where 8 eighth-notes are grouped in 3 3 2 notes to total 8.

Triad A three note chord. Usually achieved by stacking every other note in a scale for a total of three notes.

Voice Leading A term used for connecting the chord tones of one chord to another with the notes moving the least amount necessary to make the chord change. This makes a really smooth sound.

Whole-step The second smallest interval in music. It is two half-steps in distance. Most scales consist of half-steps and whole-steps.

ABOUT AUTHOR

Michael Cerulo (aka Suke) is a guitarist and multi-instrumentalist whose life long love and devotion to music has given him a very distinct and identifiable sound. Whether it's his fluid guitar melodies, the warm organic tone of his flute, or his own recordings where he plays and produces all of the music, Suke's individuality, creativity and talent are evident in all of his creations.

Born in a suburb of Boston, Suke was raised in a musical family. His grandfather (George Lane) was a composer, multi-instrumentalist and bandleader during the late 40's and early 50's. All four of George's siblings were musicians as well, often being employed in his big band. The youngest brother helped start **Berklee College of Music**. Suke began playing guitar and taking music lessons when he was twelve. Being persistent, with an unbending intent to learn and grow, he then enrolled in Berklee College of Music in Boston. After graduating in '94, while also working for MOTU music software, Suke became a full time touring musician. Suke composed, played guitar and flute with his band **Schleigho**.

Schleigho (pronounced shlay-ho) was formed at Berklee in 1993 and was touring around the country a year later. The band's style is a mix of jazz and funk, with each of its four members contributing equally to bring about an unprecedented wall of sound. Being predominately instrumental, the band's incredible talent and versatility allows them to go from opening for the Allman Brothers to playing high scale jazz venues while satisfying the most discriminating of tastes. The band released their first CD (*self-titled*) in 1995, '*Farewell to the Sun*' in 1997 and '*In the Interest of Time*' in 1998. In 2000 the band signed with **Flying Frog Records (owned and managed by members of the Allman Brothers)**. Under Flying Frog Records they released '*Continent*' in 2000, and '*Live at HoDown 2000*' the following year. Schleigho has met with great success over the years; from amassing a substantial and dedicated national following to '*Continent*' breaking into the top 20 on CMJ and college Jazz radio charts. Averaging over 200 shows annually across the country, they have shared the stage with **The Allman Brothers band, Derek Trucks, Bela Fleck, John Scofield, Karl Denson, Maceo Parker, G. Love and Special Sauce, Galactic, moe. and Soulive**, to name a few. Schleigho has performed at the JVC Jazz festival (NYC), the Gathering of the Vibes, the High Sierra Music Festival, and the Berkshire Music Festival, among others, and are veterans of the club/college circuit and large festival scene for over 20 years.

Suke also performed for years with the band **Conehead Buddha**, which is a song structured improvisational fusion of hip-hop, rock, and jazz, flirting with many styles from drum and bass to latin and reggae. It's a high energy show featuring Terence and Shannon Lynch.

Suke has been steadily involved with the production of music for multimedia. For the last twenty years Suke has been developing his production and engineering abilities in his own project studio to further enhance his musical visions. He created *Tone Over Tone* in which he composes, performs, engineers, mix's and masters recordings to be licensed for multimedia applications. This area of music production allows for infinite amounts of creation and timbre. Using conventional instruments, modern technology and a thorough musical background, Suke now creates breathtaking music that utilizes almost any instrument in creation with lush sound design.

His sound is refreshing and his performance is intense. You can always hear diverse musical influences throughout his compositions and soloing. Music from the likes of Jimi Hendrix and Van Halen to John Coltrane, Roland Kirk, and George Benson. From Jeff Beck and Ozzy to Herbie Hancock, Mingus and Miles. From Igor Stravinsky to Square Pusher and Amon Tobin.

Suke currently resides in New York City with his family and has been the *Director of Lead Guitar Program at New York City's "Best" Guitar School* since 2004. He has taught over 15,000 lessons and classes amassing a staggering amount of teaching experience. Suke is also responsible for the musical evaluations of incoming teachers and has often taught the other teachers at the school. The hundreds of students and thousands of hours teaching have help sculpt and mold the success of his teaching methods.

Whether it's playing in a group context, performing, teaching or creating and producing music, Suke always incorporates a fine balance of taste and technique with a result that's not soon forgotten. He always keeps his eye and ear to the future while respectfully paying homage to his influences and tradition.

www.SukeCerulo.com

www.LeadGuitarWorkshop.com